The R.I.S.E. Method

A How–to Guide for Designing Natural Appearing Ponds, Streams and Waterfalls

by Industry Veteran

Rick Bartel

Rival Publications, Inc.

Rival Publications, Inc.

Library of Congress Control Number: 2010931144
ISBN: 9781450713085

Graphic illustrations by Shawn Hiser
Custom creations in quality graphic design
http://www.shawnhiser.com

Cover Concept by Brion Sausser

Book Design by Cindy Graham, TC Publishing, Inc.
http://www.tcpubinc.com

 Published by RIVAL Publications, Inc.
http://www.rival.com

Legal Disclaimer

The R.I.S.E. Method

A How-to Guide for Designing Natural Appearing Ponds, Streams and Waterfalls

Written by Rick Bartel
A veteran industry expert and
Certified Master Water Feature Specialist
http://www.rickbartel.com

Table of Contents

Acknowledgements...8

About the Author...10

Introduction 12

Chapter 1 The R.I.S.E. Method.............................15

Chapter 2 Design Concepts...............................19

Chapter 3 Give Them What They Want 23

Chapter 4 Eliminating Human Influence.................27

Chapter 5 Random – Having No Specific Pattern 31

Chapter 6 Irregular – Having No Even Occurrence 35

Chapter 7 Spontaneous – Having No External Confinement 39

Chapter 8 Erratic – Having No Fixed Course.............43

Chapter 9 Height – Proper Uses of Elevation 47

Chapter 10 Depth – Effective Control of Water Volume...............51

Chapter 11 Width – Deviations in Expanse.................55

Chapter 12 Turns – Directional Diversity 59

Chapter 13 Splits – Islands Provide Opportunities 63

Chapter 14 Speed – Velocity Creates Visibility 67

Chapter 15 Sound – Adding Audible Dimensions 71

Chapter 16 Reasons for Change...79

Chapter 17 Material Placement 85

Chapter 18 Material Selection..89

Chapter 19 Material Quantities 93

Chapter 20 Material Sizes 97

Chapter 21 Material Types...101

Chapter 22 Material Shapes 107

Chapter 23 Edging Details..111

Chapter 24 Final Thoughts 119

Index 123

List of Illustrations & Photo Credits...128

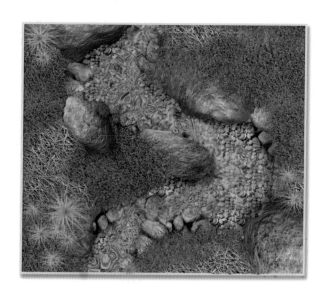

Acknowledgements

Every level of proficiency attained throughout a career is gained through a conscientious, diligent self-assessment and honest effort to further improve oneself. You need to be a self-motivated individual who truly believes that your dreams can be realized through drive and ambition, coupled with an overwhelming desire to achieve your set goals and recognize those who, throughout your life assisted you on your path to success.

Thanks to my wife, friend and life partner, Deidre, who inspired me, supported my efforts and encouraged me through the years as I perfected my craft.

Thanks specifically to Chic Kelty and Valerie Steele, who through the Savio Water Feature Institute (sponsored by Savio Engineering, Inc.) allowed me the opportunity to significantly touch the lives of thousands of industry professionals as the Administrator and Primary Instructor of this great, innovative educational institution.

Thanks also to the many professionals who blazed the trail that steered my career course, like Anthony Archer-Wills, The grandfather of our industry, and my mentor who truly launched my career with his wonderful theory of "organized chaos," stemming from a lecture back in the late 1980's. Anthony's impeccable and unparalleled insight into the naturalistic arrangement of rocks and boulders was truly refreshing. My undying thanks to the many others like Dave Duensing, Brian Van Bower, Max Hammond, Cla Allgood, David Tishman, Gary Wittstock and Kelly Billing, who along with organizations like the National Association of Pond Professionals each touched my life in various ways that helped forge my ideas into reality.

And most importantly, I'd like to thank the thousands of students around the world that have attended my lectures and seminars. You allowed me the opportunity to share my thoughts and ideas for the advancement of quality, naturalistic water feature design and installation and specifically requested the publication of the techniques outlined in this book.

Responsible Organizations and Industry Manufacturers are diligently working together to increase the level of educational opportunities available for contractors and other industry professionals. Together we can move the industry forward.

About the Author

Rick Bartel, an acknowledged veteran industry expert and Certified Master Water Feature Installation Contractor for more than twenty years, has reached nearly every milestone imaginable in this industry. As the previous owner of a design and installation business, Rick was credited with reaching the fifteen million-gallon milestone with his water feature creations worldwide. Early on in his career he demonstrated a passionate desire to advance quality water feature installations to the next level of proficiency by developing the now well-known and industry respected Random, Irregular, Spontaneous and Erratic technique for naturalistic watershaping known as the R.I.S.E. Method.

This method was so simple that beginners could easily follow along yet so advanced experienced industry veterans would also gain valuable and beneficial information. The R.I.S.E. Method installation technique, emulating nature in a most precise and significant way, has literally changed the way the world's foremost installers are currently designing water features. To date The R.I.S.E. Method has been credited with receiving more than 1,800 national and international awards and recognitions for quality water feature design and installation practices. From Design Masters competitions and the first ever NAPP Annual Service Award to being featured on Extreme Landscapes and the DIY Networks Waterscapes Workshop, The R.I.S.E. Method has literally taken water feature design to a new level.

The author of more than 300 internationally published works on the subject of quality water feature installation, Rick was adamant about sharing every piece of information he gained with others in the industry. He believes you cannot consider yourself a successful water feature contractor if you are in possession of information or knowledge not readily available to others. To share this information with his colleagues and peers put everyone on an even playing field. Then, he felt he had to work that much harder, placing equal knowledge against equal knowledge, to keep his business ahead of the competition. And yet he never considered them his competition; he often worked side by side with them on several large-scale projects as though they were colleagues.

In 2001, Rick was invited to sit on the Board of Directors for the National Association of Pond Professionals where he played a key, proactive roll for the next eight years. Concurrently, he served as the Chairman of the Continuing Education Program, the Certified Contractor Program, and co-authored their National Certification Test.

In mid-2006, Rick was approached by industry giant Savio Engineering and asked to set up and implement an innovative, think-outside-the-box educational program that became what is known today as the Savio Water Feature Institute.

In late 2007, Rick sold his water feature installation business and became the institute's full time Program Administrator and Primary

Rick Bartel, Instructor and Author

Instructor. Today, this institution offers a well-rounded curriculum of several advanced-level workshops, seminars and contractor forums designed to assist today's professionals in operating sustainable and profitable water feature installation businesses. By late 2009 more than 6,200 industry professionals had attended Rick's seminars and workshops worldwide, which have earned an unprecedented six prestigious awards for excellence in education.

Introduction

Welcome to the wonderful world of naturalistic water features. These man-made landscape and architectural environments are designed with a primary focus on water while achieving a natural resulting appearance. Naturalistic water feature applications have a multitude of phenomenal opportunities just waiting to be tapped into! We, as humans, have the power, the knowledge and the ability to reproduce most any vision we can imagine; yet the majority of water feature installations today are still being installed with outdated techniques from years past. Whether designed by a professional architect and installed by a licensed contractor or perhaps a homeowner doing a weekend project, water features can easily copy nature in a most precise way if we would only take the time to learn what actually makes something look natural. The time has come to venture out and forge ahead, exploring new and innovative methods and techniques that will capture the awesome power and appearances of nature in these landscape and architectural features. This industry has the tremendous potential to move forward in a most significant way.

Excellence Through Education

Quality classes, seminars and workshops are the solution to advancing the water feature industry beyond the out dated design and installation techniques of days gone by. The more each of us knows and fully understands about water features, the better off we all are.

The solution to this advancement: **Education!** Educate everyone! Educate the professionals, educate the businesses, educate employees and educate the homeowners. The more each of us knows and fully understands about water features, the better off we all are. Homeowners will understand there is more to it than just digging a hole and filling it full of water and expecting it to work properly. Contractors will understand they can't slap some cheap project together today while using inferior components and installation practices and expect to

be in business the following year with a list of satisfied clients. Architects will understand they can't draw a visually pleasing image on a piece of paper and expect it to work in real life applications. Water feature design and installation is not rocket science and it can be relatively simple and easy to approach if we all understood a few fundamental concepts.

One of the most frequently encountered and the single most discussed topic of dislike for any completed water feature project is the resulting appearance, or lack of aesthetically pleasing attributes. Think about it: When everything is said and done, a project's components are, or should be, fully hidden from sight. No one wants to look out over a completed water feature project site and see unsightly man-made components everywhere. It is our job and our responsibility, when installing any water feature, to adequately hide or camouflage all of these necessary yet unsightly components. The excavation, liner, pumps, filters, plumbing, etc. should all be hidden from view and we are left primarily looking at the rocks that make up the majority of today's water feature installations. So, if we hide all of these necessary components and are left looking at rocks and boulders, it stands to reason that if this rockwork is unsightly and unnatural, the project will be unsightly. And if this rockwork is absolutely awe-inspiring and naturalistic in appearance, then you should be left with a truly phenomenal water feature to be fully enjoyed by all.

This publication will provide you with all of the necessary information, focusing specifically on the elements and characteristics needed to attain truly naturalistic results in any completed project. You will learn the intricate details of what actually makes a water feature appear so natural, why these phenomenal techniques work, and how to avoid the critical design errors left over from the good old days that are still in use today. Join me as we explore the fascinating and wonderful world of water features from a naturalistic perspective that is sure to dazzle the most critical eye as we RISE to the challenge of designing and installing truly naturalistic water feature projects. Welcome to the R.I.S.E. Method.

The R.I.S.E. Method

CHAPTER

1

R. Random
Having No Specific Pattern.

I. Irregular
Having No Even Occurrence.

S. Spontaneous
Having No External Confinement.

E. Erratic
Having No Fixed Course.

The R.I.S.E. Method

The R.I.S.E. Method is an acronym, developed and perfected over many years of detailed research and study, describing the techniques used to achieve phenomenal proficiency in naturalistic water feature designs with regards to the correct selection process of quality materials and their proper placement.

The R.I.S.E. Method

R.I.S.E. is an acronym, developed and perfected over many years of detailed research and study, describing the techniques used to achieve phenomenal proficiency in naturalistic water feature designs with regards to the correct selection process of quality materials and their proper placement. This technique has been successfully utilized in

Achieving truly naturalistic results is quite simple once you understand just how nature reacts to the surrounding elements. Learning how to select the best possible materials for your water feature projects and knowing exactly how and where to place those materials, will allow you to accomplish anything.

Natural Resulting Designs

the design and installation of tens of thousands of actively operating water features throughout the world. The R.I.S.E. Method is directly responsible for an industry leading record number of local, regional, national and international awards and recognitions for some of the most natural appearing water features ever created.

Nothing in the natural world has a systematic, methodical or planned pattern, and nature appears to drift and flow almost carelessly and haphazardly from one area to another. However, upon careful examination you will discover that there are always reasons why the natural world changes, why one particular type of element exists in one area and not another, or why there are certain elements in one particular position or situation but not in others. Nature actually has a reason for everything and once you have discovered these reasons you will have the ability to recreate nature in a very precise manner, thereby creating more natural appearing landscapes and water features.

Great care has been taken to meticulously break down the multi-faceted and complex concepts of natural design into a series of very simplistic layers of elements and characteristics as they pertain to material selection and placement. Individually, some of these layered elements, characteristics and concepts, along with their corresponding graphic illustrations, may seem almost too simple. However, you must understand that the only way to truly see what makes up a natural appearance is to break everything down into the most basic layers. When you start combining each of these different elements together, you will begin to see how confusing and complicated it would be if you did not first look at and fully understand the core existence of each layer individually without the influences of other elements to cloud your perception. Once you understand and have mastered each of these key elements individually and then begin to use them in your designed creations, there will be no limit to your abilities. You will see results never before believed attainable.

Design Concepts

Design Concepts

The methods and techniques described in this book are based on several well established and recognized design concepts that look specifically at the composition of design elements, their combined interaction with one another and the techniques used to reveal the true form of each individual element. What makes the R.I.S.E design and installation method so revolutionary and unique is no one has previously simplified the concept into understandable segments of use and adequately adapted it to today's water feature design and installation applications. The particular approach that this technique uses with respect to visual organization and balance is known by many names.

Notice all of the listed proven design concepts, though not identical, are extremely similar in definition.

Natural Balance -
A Harmonious Or Satisfying Arrangement Of Parts Or Elements.

Proportional Harmonics -
Elements Properly Related To One Another In Measurable Balance.

Spacial Orientation -
The Fundamental Position Of Elements Within A Given Space.

Feng Shui -
A Pleasing Combination Of The Elements Forming A Whole.

Accepted Design Concepts

The design concepts utilized in the R.I.S.E. techniques are well established and proven methods. Once you understand how the various elements in your design react with one another, balance and harmony can be achieved, thereby allowing viewers to truly enjoy and appreciate the created space.

As outlined above in these design concepts, **all materials or elements** within a given space **do** interact with one another. Too much of one element will overpower the others. Too little of any one element within an area can make that particular element virtually non-existent or invisible as a contributing factor of balance while attempting to achieve sensory perfection. Change the layout, type, style, size, color, texture, shape or quantity of any single element or group of elements in relationship to the others within a given space and you will have effectively changed the outcome, the feel, and the mood or ambience of the entire design.

A major problem within the water feature industry and the reason for the development of the R.I.S.E. Method concept is that the vast majority of both laymen and professional installers are still designing and installing water features the same way it was done fifteen or twenty years ago. Part of this rests on the fact that available educational opportunities and published resources were so ridiculously outdated; there were no alternative options for those hungry for additional information. Times have changed and technology has changed. There are now more advanced and innovative techniques and educational opportunities readily available to contractors and homeowners alike as they pursue perfection in quality water feature installations. There is no place or logical reason for using outdated and inferior components or information in today's technologically advanced world.

Anyone installing a water feature typically would not or should not install a small 50-gallon goldfish pool with huge three or four ton boulders. Nor should they install a large 10,000-gallon water feature with the dreaded "pearl necklace effect" consisting of hundreds or even thousands of little bowling ball sized rocks meticulously and methodically lined up end to end in a single file row around the perimeter or shoreline of the water feature. (See image on next page). Yet this practice is being used every single day, only to have the installer turn around and ask why their creations do not have

"Nature actually has a reason for everything and once you have discovered these reasons you will have the ability to recreate nature in a very precise manner, thereby creating more natural appearing landscapes and water features."

Outdated Installation Techniques

It is unnecessary and unfortunate that the poorly chosen installation techniques used in the above waterfall are still used with the majority of water feature installations, yet it can take less time, effort and money to use far better methods and techniques providing far superior projects.

Unnatural Appearances

Old and outdated installation techniques are not necessarily wrong or unsightly... they just simply do not look natural. Ponds such as the one pictured above can use three to four times more rock material than what is actually necessary.

a more naturalistic appearance. The elements comprising a water feature project must be proportionally balanced with one another; they must also fit in with the overall project area. The water surface area, rocks and boulders, plant material, light and shadow, even color and texture will all play an important and intrinsic roll in the overall balanced appearance of your designs and ultimately your ability to achieve the intended end results and goals of the finished project.

Give Them What They Want

CHAPTER

3

Give Them What They Want

A key element in being successful with any project is to have the ability to provide the intended end results and give the property owner what they desire. Sometimes this is not necessarily what they want but rather what they need.

Whether you are a homeowner installing your first water feature for your spouse or a professional contractor providing a paid service to your many clients, you must be able to combine the appropriate and essential elements and characteristics that will ultimately bring the project together with the desired results. Formal water feature applications will always have their place within this industry, but the overwhelming popularity for a water feature yielding a natural appearance can no longer be ignored.

Here are a few industry facts and statistics that have been accumulated in recent years involving the popularity of naturalistically appearing water features with those who ultimately own or care for the finished projects.

- Naturalistic water features are popular throughout the world by all nationalities and with people from all walks of life. They are not specific to any one ethnicity, culture, social level or region of the world.

- Naturalistic water features are the number one item that both commercial and residential property owners want to add to their property by a margin of 3 to 1 over any other available option.

- Naturalistic water features, with an emphasis on low-maintenance substantiality and possessing a high level of water quality, can add significant value to any piece of commercial or residential property.

Over 80% Prefer Natural

Natural resulting designs such as those achieved with
the R.I.S.E. Method, are the most sought after style
desired by more than 80% of water feature owners.
This information is reflected in several recent
industry and contractor based surveys.

- Water features in general are not only soothing and relaxing but have proven, substantial health benefits to humans, backed by recent physical, biological and medical scientific research data.

- Water features with a naturalistic appearance are the single most sought after design and installation style desired by more than 80% of potential clients according to recent contractor surveys.

Naturalistic water features are popular throughout the world by all nationalities and with people from all walks of life.

It was with information such as this that the R.I.S.E. Method was originally developed and perfected. Establishing a need for a better and more efficient way to both design and install constructed ornamental aquatic features yielding naturalistic results.

Whether homeowner or professional, our collective goal is to end up with a water feature we can be proud of. Cutting corners on quality will only provide you with later disappointment. Doing it right the first time will ultimately save you time and money.

If naturalistic results are the intended goal of our projects, we must then pursue techniques that will assist us in attaining these desired results.

Eliminating Human Influence

Eliminating Human Influence

Many people have the ability to look at something and know it just doesn't look right but they don't know why. Some people can look at a particular set of objects or areas and determine one looks better than the other does. The majority of us will even agree to a fairly high degree of consistency and conformity that one particular design looks better than another – and that's good – but it's not good enough! If you want to take your water feature creations to the next level of proficiency in design advancement, you must know and understand why one option looks more natural than another! Understanding "Why" is the key to achieving that level of perfection and proficiency all of us dream of but few of us attain. Creating a truly natural appearing water feature is well within grasp as long as a few fundamentally sound principles are fully understood and followed.

Why does one water feature appear more natural than another does? Why does this waterfall look more awesome than that waterfall? In order to understand and answer these questions and more, the R.I.S.E. Method was based on the study of the only true expert: nature itself. Nature held the key to success in designing and installing truly magnificent and natural appearing man-made water features in landscape and architectural applications. As the study progressed, a pattern emerged bringing to light a series of essential elements or characteristics necessary for accomplishing the sought after and resulting goals. The process was adjusted and perfected over time only to find that the basic concept was essentially the same but the intimate and minute details of each individual project were a perpetual improvisation.

One of the most important and the very first obstacle that must be overcome is human influence. We must eliminate the effects of human influence from our naturalistic design attempts. A never-ending stream of information constantly and consistently bombards our mind by way of our senses, particularly through sight. Many of these bits of information are filled with human qualities.

Take a close look around you. Our cities and towns are filled with structures that are straight, level, plumb and square. Many of these structures will have windows or design elements that are all the same size and spaced exactly the same distance from each other. If there are any angles, curves or arcs to be seen, they are precisely calculated, measured and divided evenly to fit perfectly within a prescribed area. Fences, telephone poles and the landscape areas around our structures are all perfectly spaced, balanced and centered. Even our roads and sidewalks are all meticulously laid out with lines and joints, intersections and splits that are evenly spaced, having the exact same width or run perfectly parallel to an adjacent object. In order to truly have the ability to design and install water features with possessed naturalistic qualities, you must first have the ability to block out all of the man-made influences flowing into your mind.

Man-Made Design Influences

Everywhere we look, we are being overburdened by even, balanced, centered, straight, level, plumb and square attributes. In order to truly achieve naturalistic results, these man-made qualities need to be purged from your mind and your designs.

Forget about even, balanced, centered, straight, level, plumb and square attributes and let the natural world dictate where your properly chosen materials need to be placed within the parameters of your designed project.

Let the natural world dictate where your properly chosen materials need to be placed within the parameters of your designed project.

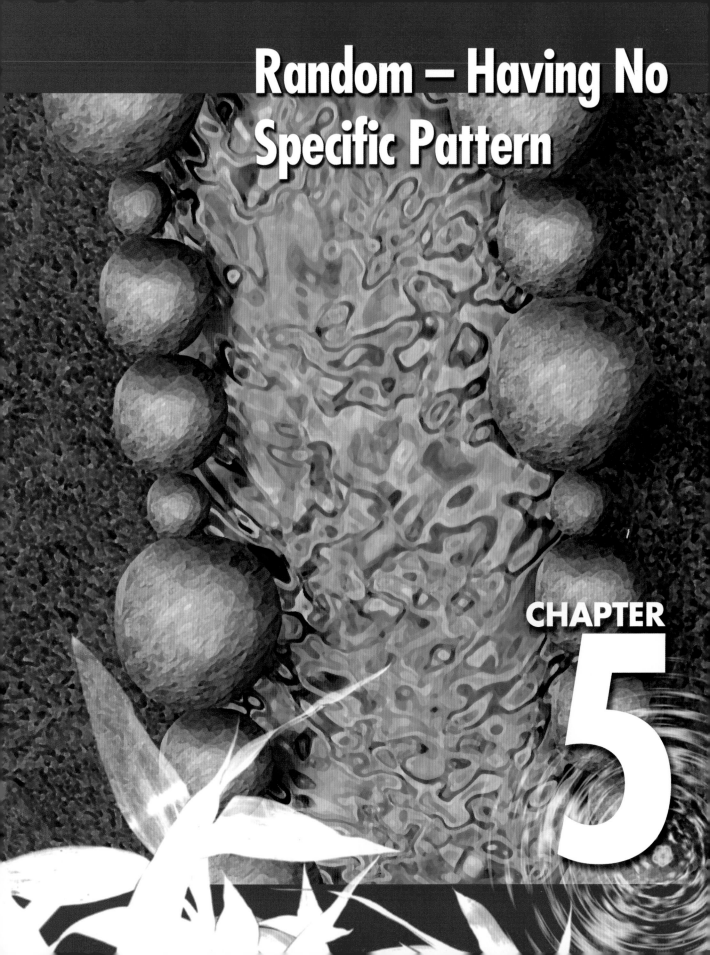

Random – Having No Specific Pattern

CHAPTER 5

Random— Having No Specific Pattern

Placing exact same sized rock in a single-file monotonous ring around the perimeter of a pond will result in the dreaded "pearl necklace" effect. Avoid this unnatural design error by following the rules of nature by not creating specific patterns in the placement of your materials.

When something is random, it has no specific pattern. The random characteristic specifically refers to the size of the materials being used in any one particular application.

You do not want to arrange same-sized objects one after the other or different sized objects into one particular order and then repeat that specific order again and again in the exact same way. If you do, you will have created a pattern, and a

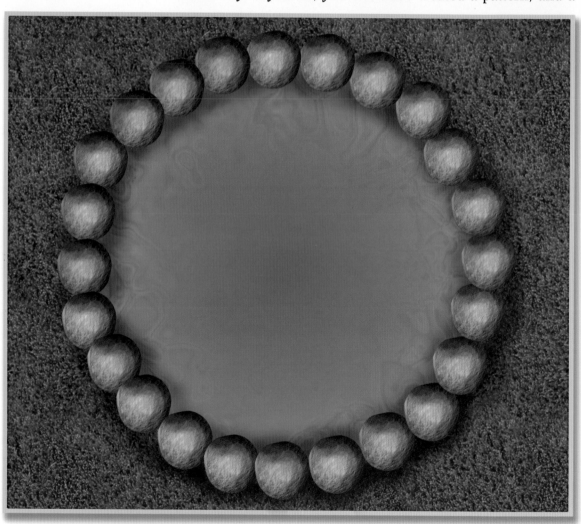

Pearl Necklace Effect

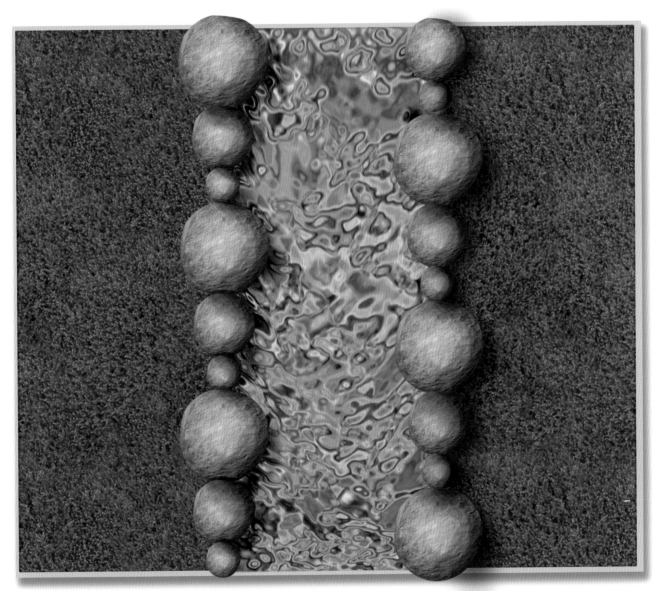

Patterned Material Placement

pattern will not appear to be within the scope of the natural realm. If your materials are the same size, you will have created what has been referred to in this industry as the "pearl necklace effect." To avoid this critical design error, you will need to obtain additional materials of the same type and quality but in different sizes to break this potential pattern. Once you have different sized items to work with, do not repeat the order of large, medium and small items in a repetitious or redundant manner.

Selecting different sizes of materials for your water feature project will certainly help in achieving more natural appearances but remember, do not repeat the various-sized items in any sort of recognizable pattern. The first step in understanding nature is to avoid patterns of repetition.

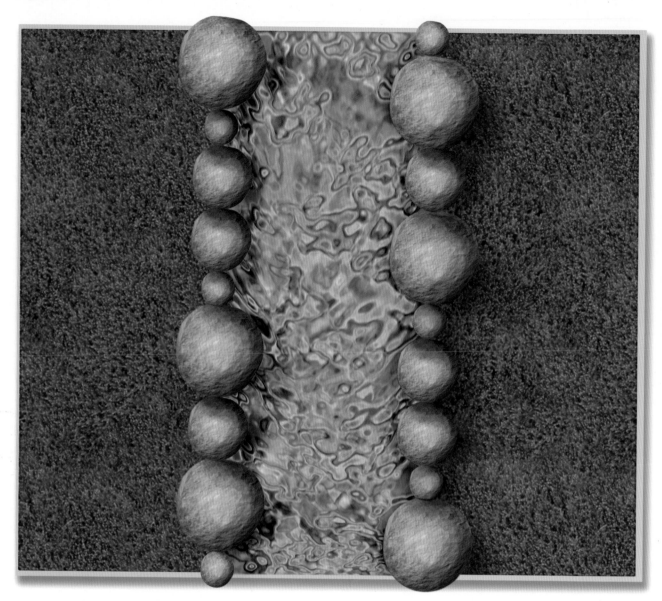

Random Material Placement

By varying the order of placement in your selected materials, you will avoid creating any sort of noticeable pattern. These unnatural patterns can be found when viewing the project site from front to back, left to right or even top to bottom. Step back from your work occasionally and view your progress from several vantage points.

Mix the sizes up and change the order of their placement so that there are no noticeable patterns of repetition based upon the size of each piece of material used. Utilizing the elements and design characteristics of the R.I.S.E. Method, you will always want to vary the order in which the different sized objects are being repeated throughout your project.

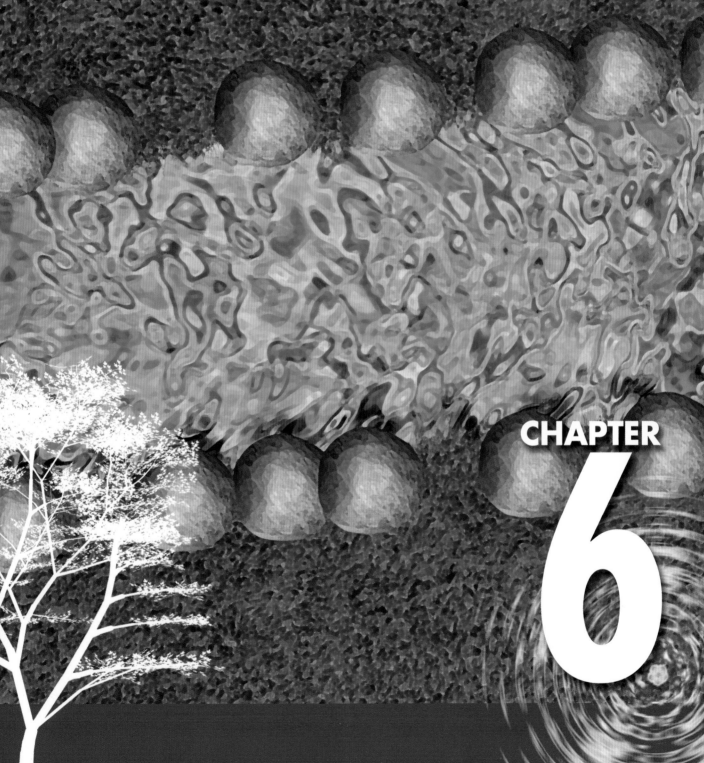

Irregular – Having No Even Occurrence

Irregular – Having No Even Occurrence

When something is irregular, it has no even occurrence. The irregular characteristic specifically refers to the spacing between each of the items and individual pieces of material being used on any project.

In nature, nothing is spaced evenly, but rather appears to have no particular regularity. Most natural settings appear to be scattered to the wind, which in fact is how many items are naturally distributed. The wind can pick up an assortment of plant seeds and deposit them in a very irregular manner, quite the opposite of the planned design of a professional landscaper.

In a natural arrangement, some objects may be touching each other while some are very close together but not touching, and still others items are more distant and further apart. The rocks and boulders, or any other material choice used in and around the various areas of your water feature projects, should possess this same irregular distribution.

Space each particular item further away from or closer to the items proceeding or following it in an irregular meandering of placement. This spacing can be done both laterally and longitudinally depending upon each specific project or design and the space available for that particular installation.

Do not allow your materials to define either the inside parameters or the outside perimeter of your water feature project. Space the materials left and right as well as forward and back. If you are spacing your materials the same distance from each other, you are once again creating a pattern that is unnatural in appearance.

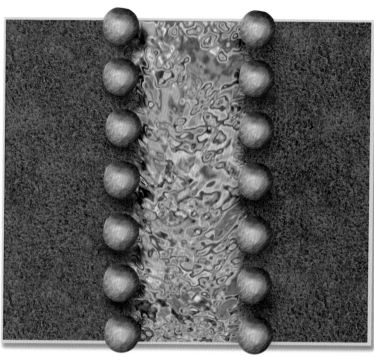

Items in Nature are never spaced evenly and exactly spaced materials in your designed water feature projects will surely set the stage for a man-made appearance in the end result. If you think your materials are too evenly spaced, they probably are.

Evenly Spaced Materials

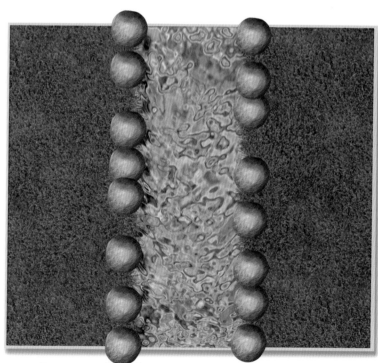

Avoiding evenly spaced materials means not making subtle changes. Make absolutely certain that some of your materials are completely touching in full contact with one another and some are close together but clearly not touching and still others are further apart from each other.

Irregularly Spaced Materials

You should not allow your material selections to define either the inside parameters or the outside perimeter of your water feature project.

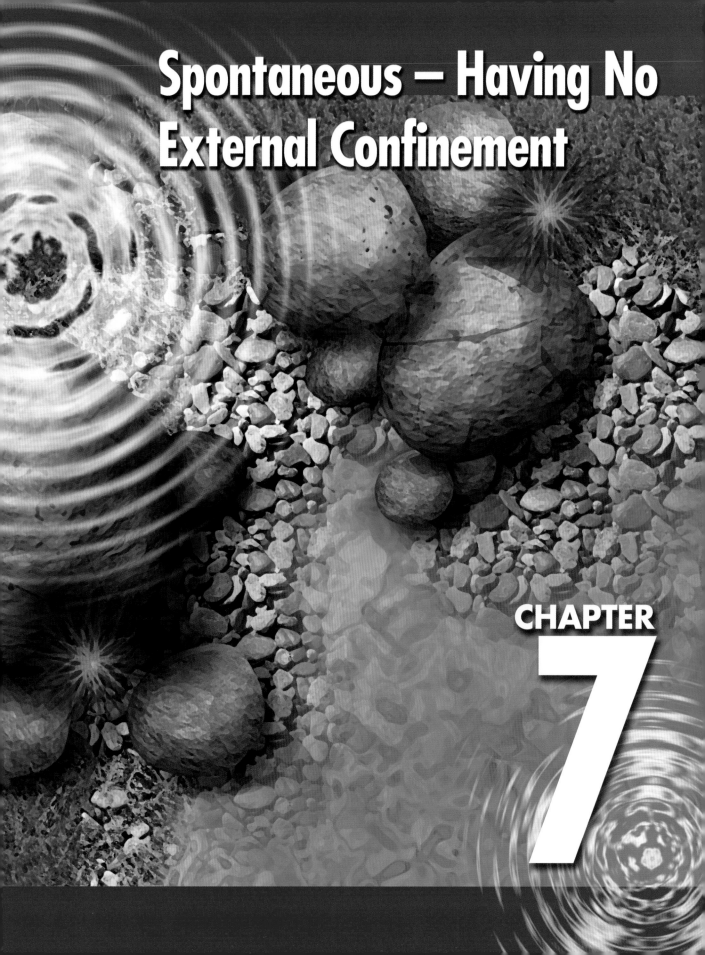

Spontaneous – Having No External Confinement

Spontaneous – Having No External Confinement

Naturalistic material placement should provide the viewer with a smooth blended transition from one particular material type to the next. If there is a clear and concise border between your selected materials, you have not given the area a truly natural appearance.

When something is spontaneous, it has no external confinement. The spontaneous characteristic specifically refers to the predictable boundaries unnecessarily fabricated through inferior designs where one type of element ends and another element would begin.

There should be no clear boundary or "edge" where two or more elements change control of any particular area. Such placement would be far too neat and clean or formal in appearance and give a clear indication of man-made control rather than natural existence. With water feature applications, you do not want a clear and concise border between the various types of materials and elements within any given area.

Let the water and shoreline mix and mingle in a seemingly and almost messy co-habitation where the various materials blur this boundary. Pond shorelines or stream banks should not be completely and meticulously lined with a monotonous end to end row of rocks or accented with continuous rows of gravel their entire length.

Confined Material Placement

Spontaneous Material Placement

Also, do not stop at the water line. Just because you are installing a water feature does not mean you should neglect the surrounding landscape. The entire overall scene needs to be an intricate blend that belongs together.

Do not let your landscape areas edge your entire water feature in a monotonous bed of none stop mulch and plant material surrounding your project. Have some areas of densely planted landscape or perhaps a grassy slope that extends all the way to the water's edge. Just as we will show you how to break up the inside edges of the water feature, you will want to vary the outside perimeter of the project site as well.

Blurring the boundary between various material types used in water feature installations will give a more natural appearing scene by removing the limits created by borders. This process should not be confined just to the water feature itself but to the surrounding area as well.

There should be no
clear boundary or "edge" where
two or more elements change
control of any particular area.
Such placement would be
far too neat and clean
or formal in appearance
and give a clear indication of
man-made control rather than
natural existence.

Erratic – Having No Fixed Course

Erratic – Having No Fixed Course

When something is erratic, it has no fixed course. The erratic characteristic specifically refers to the direction or flow the materials or elements are moving, or perceived to be moving. When designing a naturalistic pond shoreline or watercourse, you do not want the feature to flow in a patterned effect and create a straight or rigid man-made appearance.

Water does not flow in straight lines, so it is imperative to not allow this error to exist in your designs. Water mirrors and mimics every rise and fall in its surrounding environment and consequently adjusts its direction of flow accordingly. Likewise, do not allow a systematic and methodical series of predictable turns or movements. Water is turned by obstacles in its path, based upon the size, shape and density of these obstacles or their ability to erode.

Straight Fixed Watercourse

When designing a naturalistic watercourse, you do not want the feature to flow straight down a slope in a straight path and create a rigid man-made appearance. Water naturally reacts to every change in the surrounding topography, adjusting itself to every rise and fall while changing course around immovable objects.

Following an erratic characteristic, you should allow your watercourse to get narrower and wider, deeper and shallower, turning left and right, constantly changing and shifting in a never ending and totally unpredictable manner.

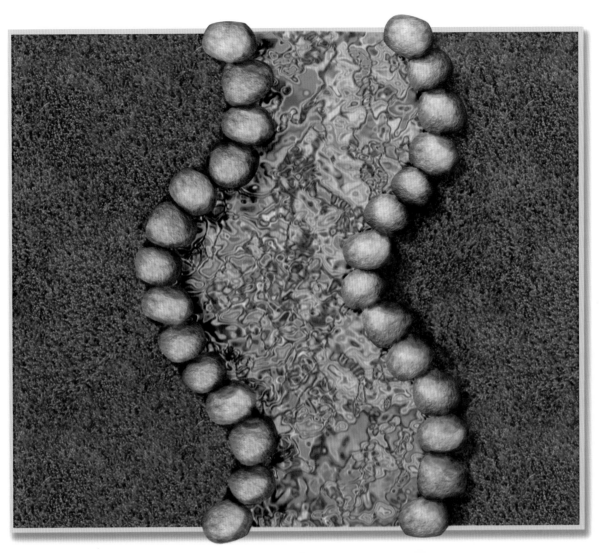

Winding Fixed Watercourse

You should not be able to predict which direction any water feature boundary is going to flow or turn simply by the limitations set from a project site's components or confinement. These erratic characteristics should only be controlled or defined by your design and the actual changes in direction should be determined by changes in the surrounding elements and materials that must give a credible explanation to these changes.

While attempting to provide naturalistic twists and turns in a designed watercourse, do not create a systematic and methodical series of predictable turns. One turn should not have the same degree of directional change, length of run or radius as any preceding or following turn.

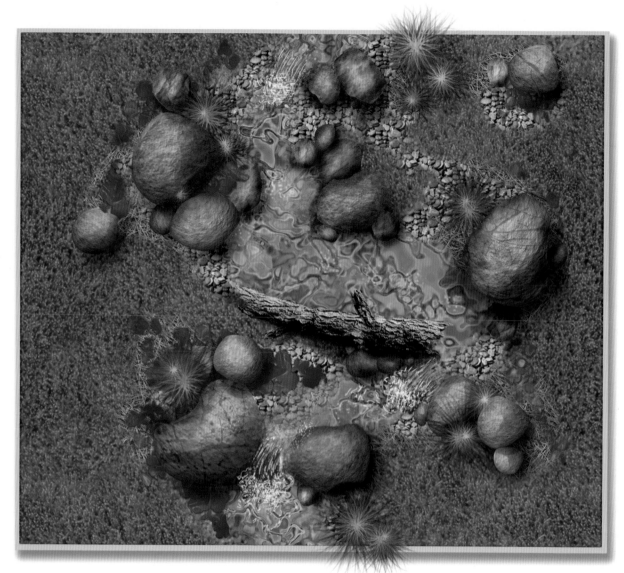

Erratic Watercourse

A naturalistic watercourse should get narrower and wider, deeper and shallower, constantly shifting and changing, molding itself to the surrounding environmental obstacles that may be blocking or altering its path. This shifting of direction, width and speed must not only be present but must also be believable by providing a reason for these changes.

Height – Proper Uses of Elevation

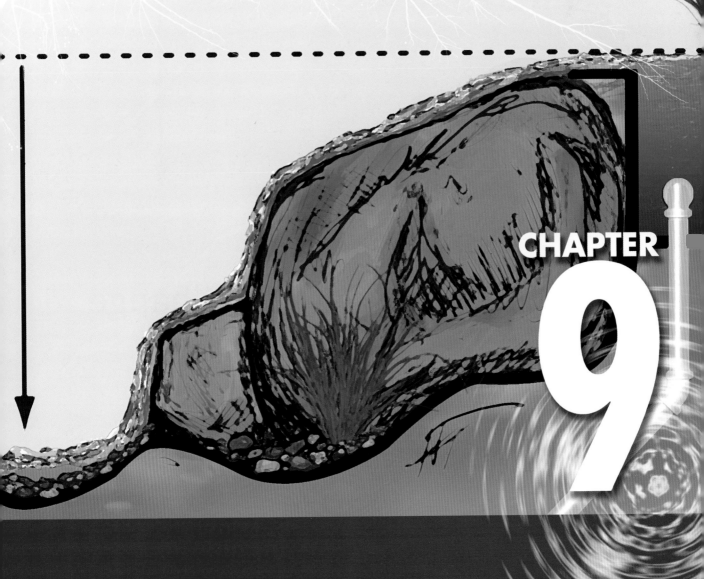

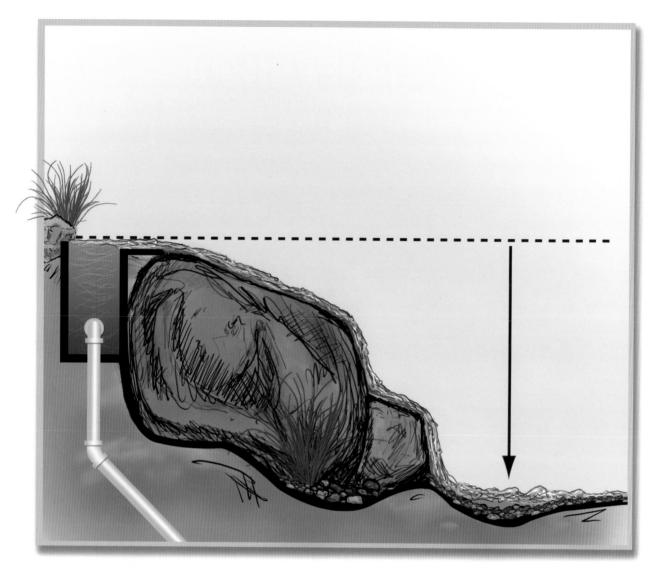

Effective Elevational Change

It is not necessary to design huge amounts of elevational change into a water feature site in order to provide sufficient slope for waterfalls or for creating high rates of flow and white water hydraulics. Awesome hydraulics can be created with relatively slight but effective elevational changes in the surrounding grade.

Height – Proper Uses of Elevation

Elevation changes above the surface of the water will add dimension and dramatic character to any feature by introducing an element of height to your project. It is important to remember that subtle changes in elevation can be quite effective if properly utilized. Particularly, when dealing with project sites where gradual elevation changes or extremely flat and level conditions pre-exist.

Nothing will look more out of place than a waterfall with a four or five-foot drop in elevation on a perfectly flat piece of property. There should always be a significant amount of landmass behind any rise in elevation or at least the created illusion that a landmass exists. These "illusions" can be camouflaged quite effectively with an appropriate landscape theme.

Remember: natural is making something look like it belongs by actually having a reason for its existence; your creation must have credibility in its existence and blend in to its surroundings. The resulting design should not stick out like a sore thumb. Commonly referred to as the "volcano effect," piling up a bunch of rocks in an unsightly landscape blemish with water spewing from the top will not give you the desired results of a natural appearing waterfall.

Water does not flow from the crest of hills in nature so we should not allow this error to reside in our constructed water feature projects.

The changes in elevation for your project must fit the surrounding lay of the land or at least produce the illusion of belonging within the immediate topography surrounding your project site.

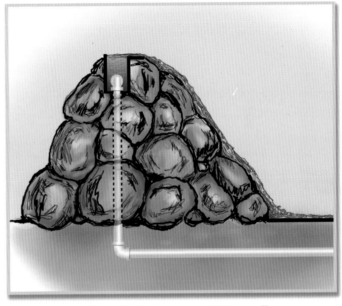

The "Volcano Effect"

Piling up a bunch of rocks, several feet high, in an unsightly landscape blemish with water spewing from its top will not give you a desired naturalistic result. Water does not naturally flow from the crest of a hill so we should not allow this error to reside in our constructed projects. This overly elevated waterfall technique is particularly out of character on flat pieces of property.

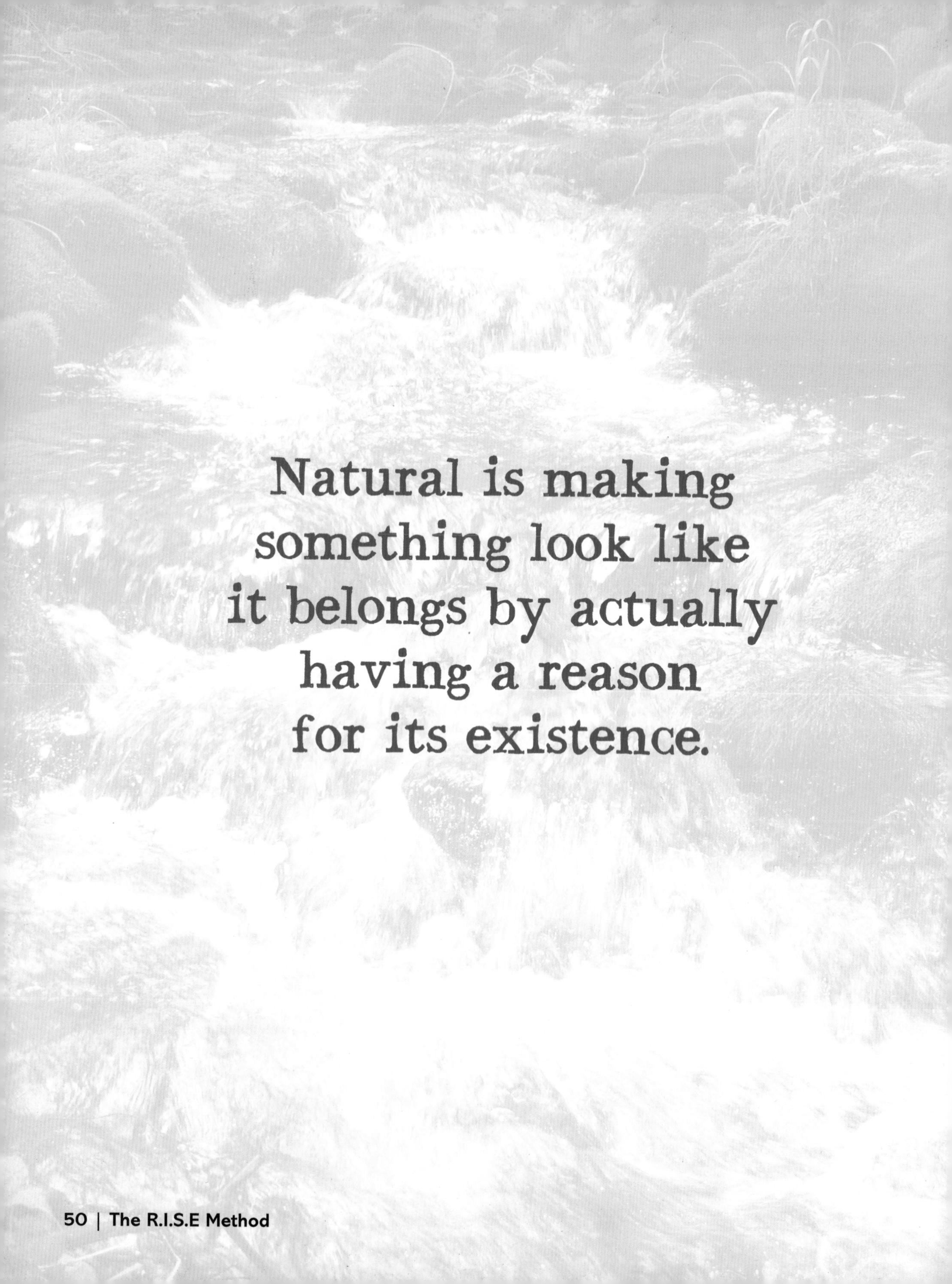

Natural is making
something look like
it belongs by actually
having a reason
for its existence.

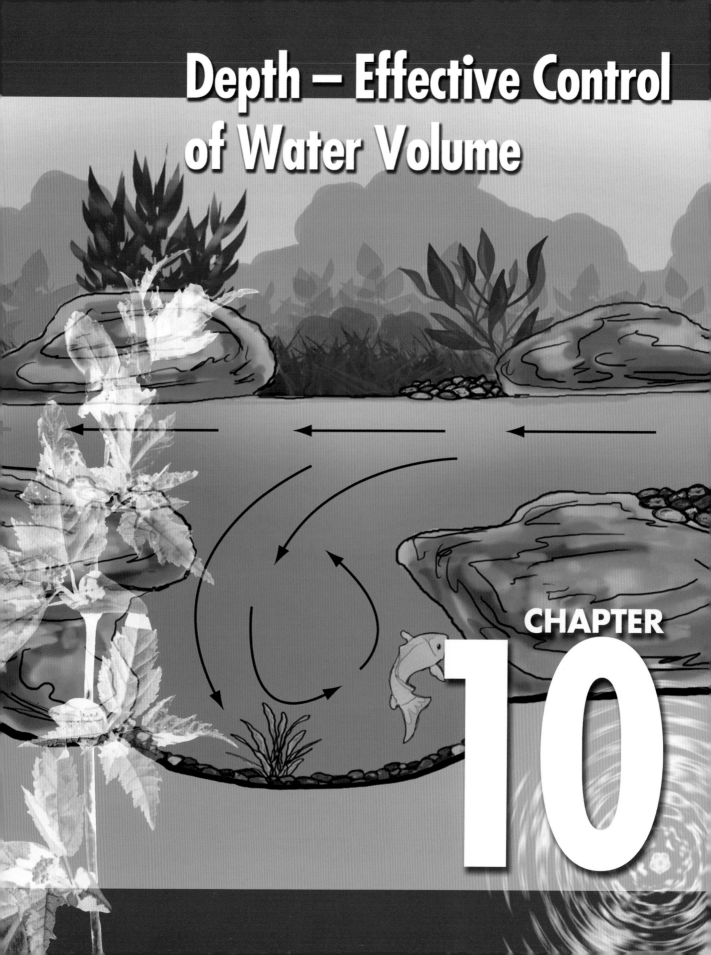

Depth – Effective Control of Water Volume

CHAPTER 10

Depth – Effective Control of Water Volume

It is important to remember to change and adjust the elevation below water level as well, adding a dimension that can truly affect the visual balance in your final project. Depth variations can be achieved through the addition of pools and shallows within the confines of the water. It would be a very boring design if a section of stream had the exact same depth throughout its entire length or a pond were precisely the same depth from one end to the other.

It is important to adjust the elevation below water level as well, adding a dimension that can truly affect the visual balance in a final project. A deep water canyon, in an otherwise shallow stream or pond, can be very appealing to both human viewers and aquatic life forms, providing a safe haven to protect and house your pond inhabitants.

Deep Water Canyon

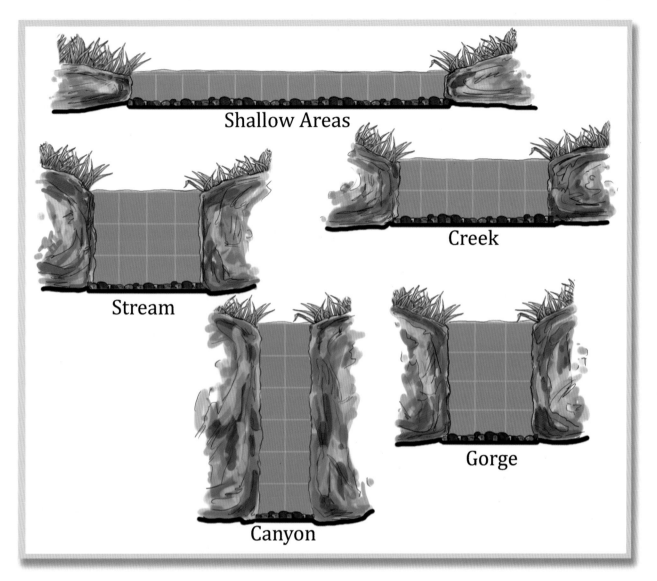

Shallow Areas

Stream

Creek

Canyon

Gorge

Reconfigured Volume

An awesome deep-water canyon can make a water feature very appealing to both human viewers and wildlife visitors, providing a safe haven to protect and house the natural inhabitants in your system. Keep in mind that some wildlife species prefer slower water and others like fast water or shallow water versus deep water.

Notice that the squared area covered by the mass of the water has not changed, yet the amount of surface area in contact with the water changes from one configuration to the next. This increased surface area raises the level of friction and thereby alters the speed with which the water can move through each of these areas.

Aquatic plants as well have specific requirements, as most are depth sensitive, thriving in a particular depth or range of water depth.

These deep-water areas are great for keeping water at consistently cooler temperatures during peak summer months; this is also a great deterrent that can effectively assist in the control of green water algae. As well, these pools and canyons can provide deep-water protection from the formation of ice during winter months.

The depth of a watercourse is controlled considerably by the dimensional configuration of the water's volume. If your water volume has not changed, the depth of the water is forced to adjust within the bounds of any changes in the shape of your watercourse. The speed with which water can pass through these areas is based on the angle of descent in the waters elevational drop and from any confinement created by restrictive edging materials.

It is important to note here that even though the actual volume of water has not changed, the friction created by the edge materials can vary, based upon the amount of actual exposed material surface area in relationship to the water. This variation in friction will affect the speed of the water and therefore affect the audible sounds of the water as well. You must keep this in mind if you design any deep pools and canyons into the parameters of your project.

Variety is the overall solution to addressing the multiple needs within any naturalistically constructed environment. Visual enhancements, wildlife habitat, natural algae control, ice control, aquatic plant placement, water speed and variations in sound are a lot of reasons to consider adjusting the depth in your water feature installations for ultimate visual perfection. Providing these various depths within your designs will undoubtedly give you greater opportunities.

Width – Deviations in Expanse

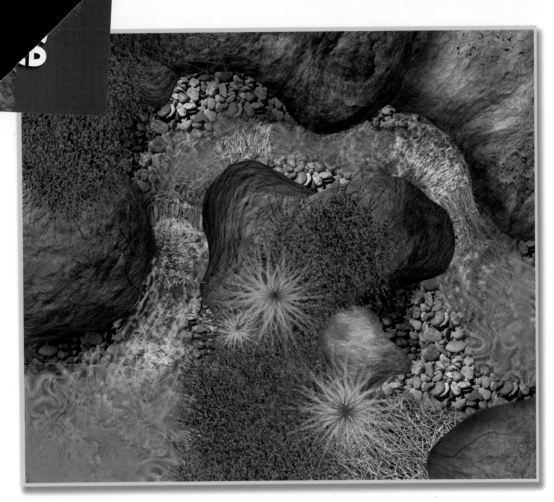

Narrow Canyons

Forcing large amounts of water through relatively narrow spaces between boulders and other solid objects can create significant amounts of whitewater with awesome hydraulic turbulence. This turbulent action can dramatically affect the sights and sounds of your designed systems by creating additional visual and audible appeal.

Width – Deviations in Expanse

Variable widths in any watercourse are essential to achieving naturalistic results and effects. One of the largest and most frequently committed errors during the installation of a watercourse is having the system remain the exact same width from one end of a watercourse to the other. This does not happen in nature or under natural conditions, so why then are we using this practice in our constructed features?

Natural streams and creeks get wider and narrower, shifting and constantly changing, following the contours of the surrounding land, adjusting direction around any large immovable objects and never staying constant or consistent. By changing the width of your watercourse, you can also effectively adjust the speed and depth of the water.

If the water volume does not change when entering into a narrow channel, the depth and speed of the water will have to change in order to accommodate this shift in mass. Forcing large amounts of water through a relatively narrow gorge or canyon can create significant amounts of whitewater with awesome hydraulic turbulence and action, thereby dramatically increasing the available range of sounds emitted by the water.

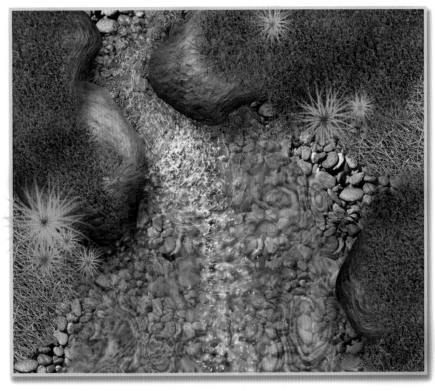

Wide Shallows

In contrast, allowing the water to spread out over a very wide area can create calming effects of rippling shallows. Be cautious in applications such as this so that you do not create extremely shallow areas with significantly slow water movement, as this action could allow the water to warm dramatically.

Slow-moving shallow water with warm temperatures can provide optimal conditions for increasing unwanted algae production.

Allowing the water to spread out over a very wide area can create calming effects of soothing, rippling shallows. Use caution with this technique as shallow, slow moving water tends to warm easily and these conditions in conjunction with other elements can assist in the increase of unwanted algae production.

Natural streams and creeks get wider and narrower, shifting and constantly changing, following the contours of the surrounding land, adjusting direction around any large immovable objects and never staying constant or consistent.

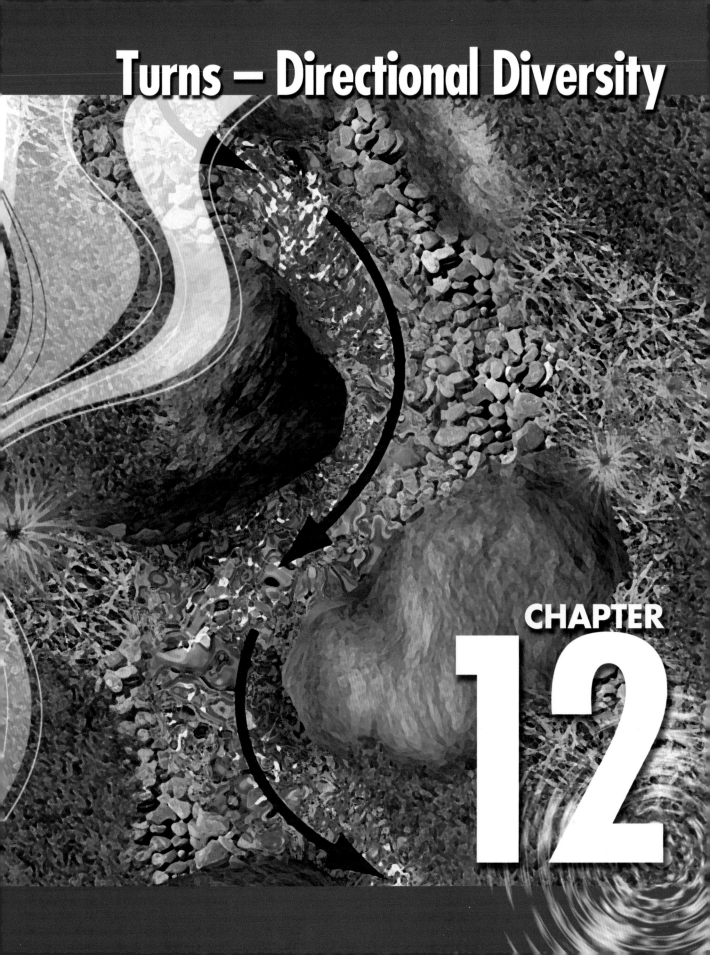

Turns – Directional Diversity

CHAPTER

12

Turns – Directional Diversity

Twists and turns must be exaggerated almost to extremes to give a naturalistic flair to your shoreline and/or watercourse. Throughout the installation process, designed turns in the water's meandering direction can appear quite significant at first and then become less and less prominent as details are added with materials, such as small rocks, gravel and aquatic plants.

Water will tend to cut the corners in its desire to take the path of least resistance, not unlike a race car straightening out the curves on a fast racecourse. This situation can be remedied by over-exaggerating your turns to allow for this occurrence. When designing any turns, particularly within any applications involving a moving watercourse such as a white-water stream or creek, you must push the limits and boundaries for phenomenal results.

Extremely exaggerated turns will force the water to change direction, since it can no longer travel in a straight path. This will also provide additional opportunities for pronounced water hydraulics and turbulence created by these changes in direction. These areas of turbulence will increase the watercourse's ability to naturally filter, provide additional dissolved oxygen levels for enhanced water quality, and increase the desired sights and sounds of moving water.

Use extreme caution when designing a pond shoreline with sharp or long-sweeping turns or other prominent changes in direction, so as not to create areas void of sufficient current, resulting in stagnant water.

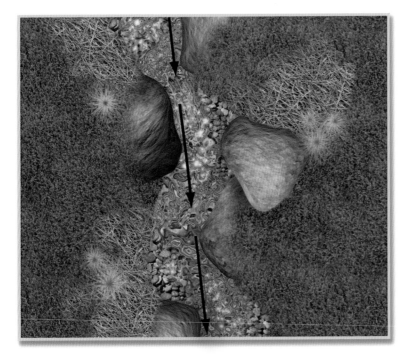

Water will tend to cut corners in its desire to always take the path of least resistance, not unlike a race car straightening out the curves of a fast race course. You may think you have created sufficient twists and turns in your designed watercourse but the waters actual path can certainly alter our perception as the watercourse fills to capacity.

Water Cuts Corners

Extremely exaggerated turns will force the water to change directions, since it can no longer physically move in a straight line. These methods work great in watercourse applications but should be used sparingly in pond shorelines as these exaggerated turns could possible create "dead" zones of stale or stagnated water.

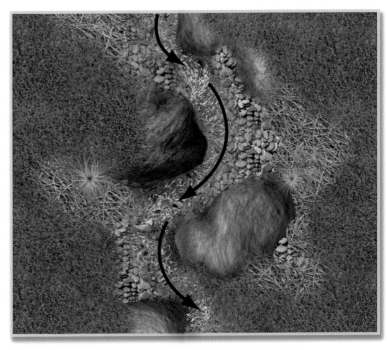

Over-Exaggerate Turns

Not only does a naturalistic watercourse need twists and turns but these turns need to possess a different angle or radius of turn and distance of run so that one turn does not look like the previous.

Splits – Islands Provide Opportunities

CHAPTER

13

Splits – Islands Provide Opportunities

Splitting the flow of a stream or dividing a waterfall or separating the surface of a pond with an island or other obstruction can be a wonderful way to add diversions, diversity and dimension to any water feature. Watercourse splits can even change vertically as well, where one side remains constant in elevation and the other side may make a dramatic change or drop in elevation.

When designing an island within the parameters of your project, be sure that it is truly an island and not just a rock strategically placed in the water. A rock placed in a stream or pond is perfectly fine, provided you understand it is not an island. Many times a rock or a nice mossy log will do just fine to separate and adjust the flow of a babbling brook. An island, however, should be an obvious and significant structure, consisting of several elements or complex combinations designed to create a substantial obstacle or diversion in the waters movement.

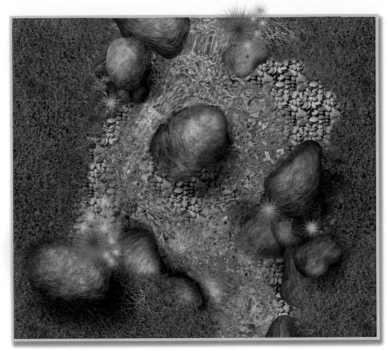

Single Rock Diversion

A single rock of most any size is a perfectly acceptable technique when placed strategically in a watercourse. This use of rock can assist in altering the actual speed and direction of the water passing through any area. However, it must be pointed out here that a single rock is not an island and should not be referred to as one.

A good suggestion for the proper installation of an appropriate island structure would be to use two or three rocks of various sizes and maybe a planting pocket with an assortment of marginal plants and a nice piece of driftwood or a small mossy branch. Fill the spaces in and around these items with small,

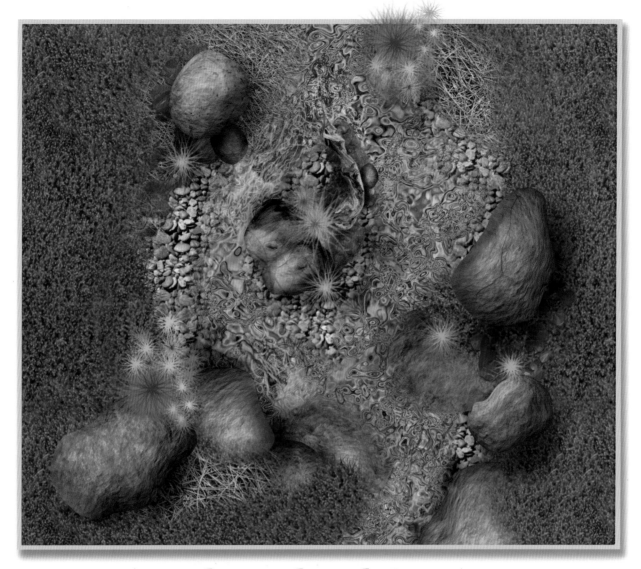

Complex Island Structure

rounded river gravel and mulch to finish off the island. This creates a significant structure that can truly be called an island. These islands and splits can be used not only for creating additional dimension to your features but will also be of use in the control or adjustment of both the direction and speed of the waters' flow and add safe havens for wildlife visitors.

A well-developed concept of an actual island structure should consist of three to five individual elements all combined together to form the island. Several rocks of various sizes, a planting bed with a variety of plant material all topped off with pockets of mulch and gravel and a mossy log or driftwood branch could certainly be called an island structure.

A single rock of
most any size is a
perfectly acceptable
technique when
placed strategically
in a watercourse.

Speed – Velocity Creates Visibility

CHAPTER 14

Speed – Velocity Creates Visibility

Two significant attributes in water feature popularity are the sight, and the sound of moving water. The visual aspect of water is created by movement with a noticeable velocity. Water velocity or the speed with which the water moves through a particular space within your water feature can be controlled in a variety of ways depending on whether you're dealing with a pond or a watercourse application.

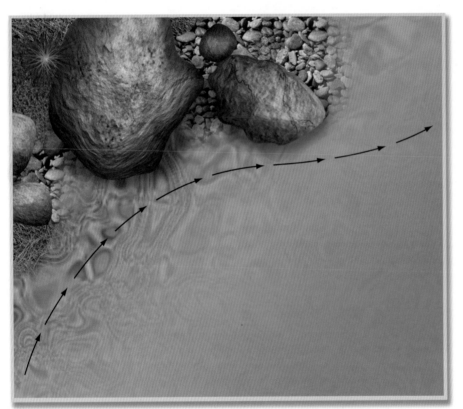

Low Ratio Movement

The current in any body of water is controlled by any obstacles that may be present. An object along the shoreline of a pond will alter the path of the waters' movement but this change will be very slight based upon the ponds' overall volume and surface area in relation to the amount of the existing flow or current.

The water velocity of a pond will be most significantly controlled based upon its total overall volume in relation to the actual speed of the current passing through it. The larger a body of water, the less noticeable any movement would be.

All lakes and ponds have currents but they are not as noticeable as the current in a stream or creek because of the increase in overall volume in relationship to the amount of water movement or volume to water current ratio.

The current in a pond will be controlled by any obstacle in its path or variation in the shoreline, but the actual water movement will be slight, based upon the ponds overall volume and surface area in relationship to the amount of existing flow rate.

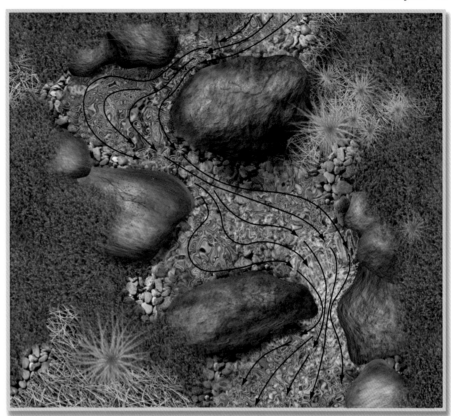

High Ratio Movement

A stream, however, can show a significant amount of water velocity because the volume to water current ratio is usually increased dramatically. These areas of extreme turbulence can be very noticeable as the water is forced through narrower passages, while being less obvious as they move through wider areas. These variances can provide a wide arrangement of hydraulic conditions with extreme beneficial results towards the sought after sights and sounds from the moving water. A stream can also be significantly faster depending upon the rate of fall in the surrounding topography.

Water running down steep grade will obviously move much faster than water on a gentle slope. This is based on friction, which is created by the length of time the water is in contact with a particular surface and the type of surface area the water must pass over as it moves through an area. The overall quantity of exposed edge materials, the types of materials used and the length of time the water is in full contact with these materials will affect the speed of the water based upon the amount of friction produced.

A watercourse can show a significant change in the level of water velocity because the water current ratio is typically increased dramatically. These areas of extreme turbulence can be very noticeable as the water is forced through narrower passages while maintaining the same water volume and being less obvious as it passes through wider areas.

Elevational Influences on Velocity

Ground slope or grade, will not only control water velocity but also water depth. The level of friction applied to the waters' surface is greater on a slight downhill slope than that of a steep incline. Because of this change in friction and gravitational pull, the water will move either faster or slower and thereby change the depth of water building up behind various objects.

It is important to remember to consider all of these aspects when designing your water feature system so as not to overflow the boundaries of the lined containment. The vast majority of moving water losses in steep slope conditions is generally due to the fact that the contained restrictions for the system are not adequate enough to control the steep descent of the water.

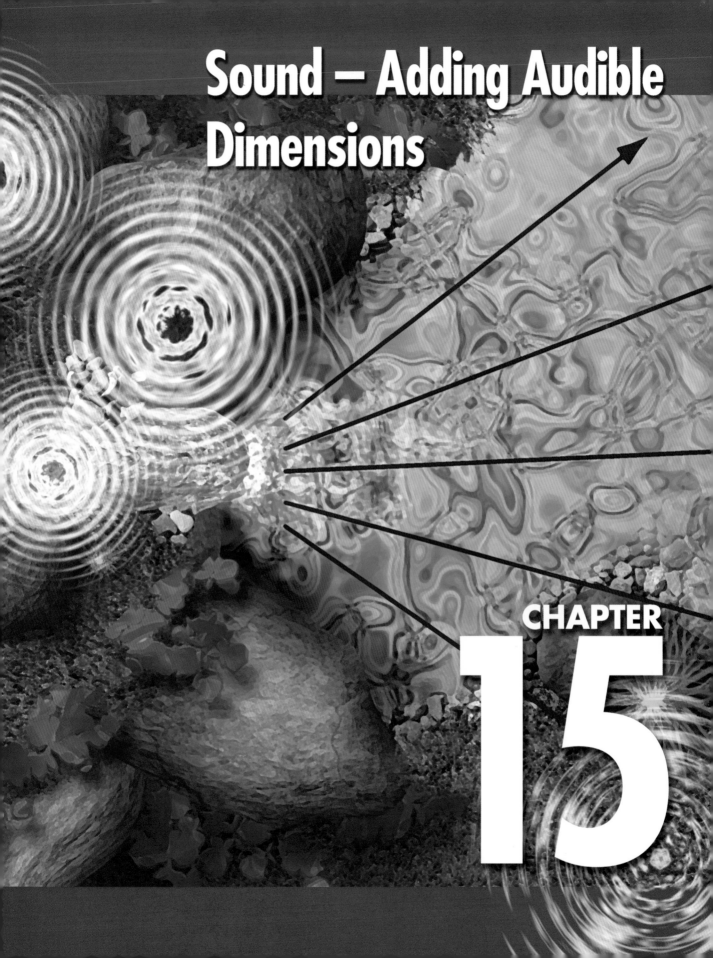

Sound — Adding Audible Dimensions

Changing the sound emitted by the waters' movement in any water feature application is as easy as changing the objects being struck by the water. High range tones can be controlled or adjusted by varying the amount of water that falls onto a solid object such as a rock. High range tones are known for drowning out unwanted noises such as nearby passing traffic.

Sound – Adding Audible Dimensions

Creating pools of varying diameters and depths within your project will not only provide wonderful opportunities for the enjoyment of wildlife and great locations for a selection of aquatic plants, but can also add a significant audible

Water Falling On A Solid Surface

Controlling Splash

dimension to your project. The actual depth and diameter of these pools will not only change the speed with which the water flows but will significantly alter the sounds emitted by the water's movement; this will allow you to audibly fine-tune your water creations.

Water splash can be responsible for large amounts of water loss in a water feature. Controlling splash can be easy if you allow a minimum of three to four feet of distance for every foot of elevational drop in water falling onto a solid surface. Two to three feet of distance will contain the splash from water falling into a small pool of water.

Water Falling Into A Shallow Pool

Control and adjust your mid-range tones when you allow water to fall into a shallow pool of water immediately following a waterfall or series of rapids. The actual diameter and depth of these small shallow pools will vary the sound emitted by the water. These mid-range tones are known for being some of the most pleasant sounds produced by water.

Control or adjust the high range tones within your water features when you allow water to fall onto a solid surface such as a rock or boulder. The amount of water you allow to fall and the distance the water actually falls will greatly effect its sound and its ability to splash.

To control any potential splash, always allow a minimum of three to four feet of distance for every foot of elevational drop onto any solid surface.

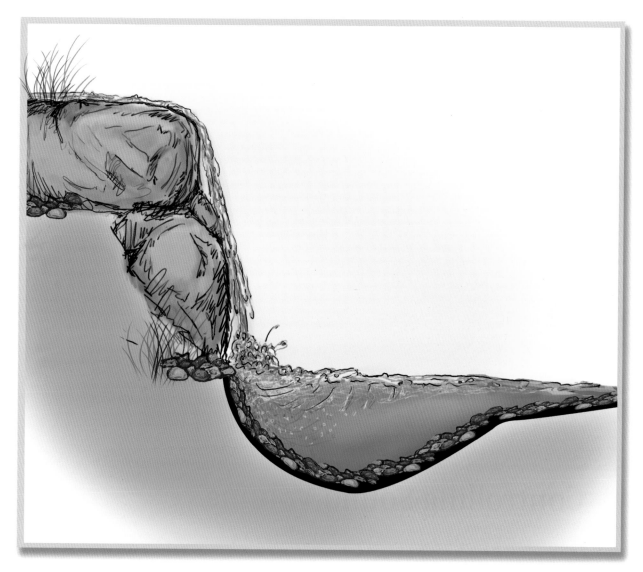

Water Falling Into A Deep Pool

Control and adjust your mid-range tones when you allow water to fall into a shallow pool immediately following a waterfall or a series of white-water rapids. Water falling into a pool does not have as great a capacity to splash as water falling onto a solid surface, so a minimum of two to three feet of distance will adequately control each foot of elevational drop in this application.

Low range tones can be produced when allowing water to fall into deeper pools of water. The actual diameter and depth of these pools will significantly alter the sounds produced by the falling water. These low range tones are known for carrying for long distances and can be of use when trying to project sound to a distant viewing area.

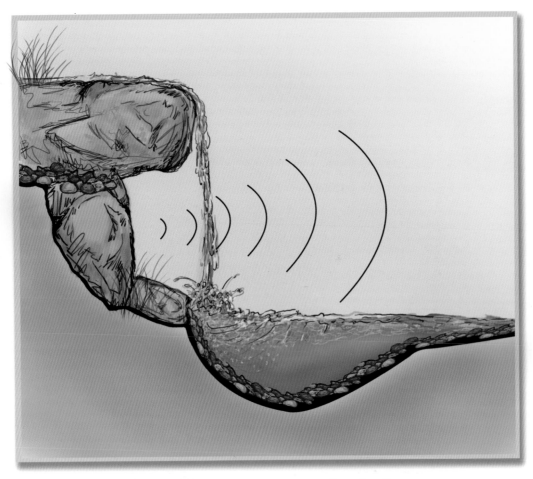

Controlling Sound Volume

The volume of sound produced by a water feature can be enhanced with the use of an echo-chamber. These echo-chambers are nothing more than a constructed amphitheater located directly behind a waterfall. These hollow chambers allow the sound waves to bounce back in the direction desired and can increase the sounds emitted by a relatively small water feature.

Low range tones can be adjusted and controlled as you allow water to fall into a much deeper pool of water. The actual depth of the pool as well as its overall diameter will ultimately dictate the sound the water emits as it hits the surface of the pool.

The type and size of material used to edge these pools will also give some control in the sound of the water as the sound waves bounce off of these placed materials, affecting the volume or level of sound produced. Placing your materials in positions that create small caves or echo chambers in or behind a waterfall can really enhance the waterfall's volume. These "echo chambers" can be quite effective in volume control.

Controlling Sound Direction

This technique can also be used to control the direction of the sound's travel. A solid backdrop of rocks and boulders can deflect the sound outward to a distant area where a visitor may otherwise be unable to hear the movement of the water.

Echo-chamber techniques can also be used in controlling sound direction by allowing you to "throw" the sound in another direction to further enhance the enjoyment capabilities of a feature. This technique works well when a water feature is viewable from one area but you wish to hear the running water in another area by bouncing the sound waves.

Creating pools of varying diameters and depths within your project will not only provide wonderful opportunities for the enjoyment of wildlife and great locations for a selection of aquatic plants, but can also add a significant audible dimension to your project.

Reasons for Change

Reasons for Change

All of the previously discussed installation methods and techniques must follow one very simple and basic rule; whether changing elevation, width, direction or depth, *ALL* changes must have a reason for existing. The edge of a natural pond will not run in a straight line or in a prescribed and designed curve but rather follow the rise and fall of the surrounding landmass, finding its optimal water level as it molds itself to the available grade.

At times these changes and adjustments may seem erratic in appearance but actually shift for very specific reasons. Once you discover and adopt these "reasons" into your project designs, your water features will take on a very credible and believable existence. Every time water changes direction or the shoreline of a pond is altered, there must be a reason for this movement or shift in direction. If you do not provide this reason for change in your designed features, you will have failed in providing a truly believable and natural appearing result.

Boulder Diversion

No matter which direction the water is moving or if the water changes direction, you must provide a believable reason why this change has occurred. There must be something such as a large immovable object to give the viewer a reason to accept the fact that the water is no longer the same shape or is no longer traveling in the same direction or speed.

Topographical Diversion

An immovable object such as a large boulder in the water's path, will most certainly alter the direction of a watercourse or pond shoreline. Even a shift in the surrounding elevational grade level will alter the waters surface or direction of flow, provided the landmass is sufficient enough to over-power the amount of water present.

Providing the viewer of a water feature with unquestionable proof of a shift in either the shape or movement of water can be accomplished with an increase in the surrounding landmass. If the ground level builds up significantly on one side of a pond, this increase in soil mass will replace the space once occupied with water mass.

Elevational Contouring

Watercourses are also controlled by their surroundings and proof must be present for viewers to comprehend why moving water has changed directions in flow. The obstacles providing these changes must be able to withstand erosion from the waters movement or the object will simply be washed away, allowing water to continue on it original path.

A simple change, such as the angle or direction of decent in the surrounding topography can also alter the path of water. The change in directional descent must be sufficient enough based upon the volume or flow of water. The more intense the water flow, the more dramatic the change must be to cause this shift in directional flow.

Streams and creeks in a natural setting do not run in a straight line; they twist and turn not at random, but rather for a very specific reason. A stream will not, or should not, change direction just because there is a bunch of small stones lined up in an arc or around a curve. In most cases the force of the water will have passed right through these inefficient barriers and obstacles, continuing on in its original path.

This elevational contouring can be a driving force in altering the direction the water can or will move. In addition, large vegetation such as trees can alter the waters' path but remember the soil around the base of the tree must appear to be protected from the force of the water.

In nature, water will erode away the soil, exposing the trees' roots and eventually the tree will topple allowing the water to resume its original path or direction. Keep this in mind when installing large plant material next to your water's edge and provide the appearance of soil stability to protect the plants roots from the illusion of erosion with a boulder, large rocks or a nice mossy log. These listed examples or other natural appearing occurrences must be present to lend credibility to the shift in movement or direction of flow in your created features.

If you decide to allow your watercourse to spread out in a wide configuration, there must be a reason as well. A very flat surrounding landmass or the stream bank being void of material of any sufficient size to adequately contain the water would thereby allow the water to spread out.

Remember always that water takes the path of least resistance and if there is a way out of its confinement, water will find it. Use these natural rules of containment and your designs will take on a completely natural appearance, simply because you have provided a reason for change.

Natural installation methods
and techniques must follow
one very simple and basic rule;
whether changing elevation,
width, direction or depth,
ALL changes must have
a reason for existing.

Material Placement

Material Placement

The preceding chapters have covered the detailed process of properly placing the appropriate materials into your water feature projects in an attempt to achieve naturalistic appearances. However, it would be difficult to fulfill these placement requirements if you were not first selecting the proper materials for use.

Material placement has covered topics from patterns, spacing and confinement, to height, depth and width of your feature, each adding a different element or dimension. All of these elements, combined together, will determine the speed and turbulence of the water. This will then affect the sights and sounds of your completed project.

Any one of the previously suggested placement techniques will assist you in improving the naturalistic appearances in your projects but the real advantages will be discovered when you have mastered all of these methods and begin combining them together for truly amazing results, emulating nature in a very precise manner!

To further advance your proficiency in achieving a truly naturalistic outcome in design and installation, we will introduce you to the reasons why the selection of the correct and appropriate materials is so important. With a certain level of skill, any materials can be used to net results that will be good or fair in appearance. If you want absolutely awesome results, attention to detail in the selection process of your materials is the answer. You must understand what makes these materials appropriate to use, why they will make a difference and what they provide that will give your projects a natural appeal.

The following chapters are not hard and fast rules but merely an aid to assist you in this selection process.

There are always exceptions to every rule; you may also find it extremely difficult or cost prohibitive in certain circumstances to acquire the necessary materials you would prefer to use. Perhaps in some instances it will not be beneficial or appropriate to purchase and/or ship the necessary materials to your project site. In these situations, you may be forced to use what is readily available, but always remember to at least attempt to locate and use those materials that will give you the optimal desired end results for your specific project.

When thinking about
what materials to use
consider texture,
color, character-lines,
moss and lichen.

Material Selection

CHAPTER

18

Material Selection

Selecting the correct rock and boulder material is very important, especially when dealing with surface appearances. The surface characteristics of your rocks and boulders can make the difference in making your water feature system appear to have been in place for a hundred years or whether it has just been recently relocated into this new location. Ancient moss-covered boulders will give your projects an appeal that can not be ignored.

Texture

Texture is a most important quality for your rocks. Many people like the appearance of freshly broken rocks and boulders because it unveils the brightly colored center of the stone not yet faded by exposure from wind, sun, erosion and abrasive weather conditions. But fresh breaks in your rocks give that man-made appearance since most of these breaks are the result of poorly used harvesting techniques at the stone quarries. In addition, these freshly broken surfaces usually yield sharp jagged edges that can be extremely damaging to many lined water features. Naturally appearing, old, worn and weathered surfaces and edges can make a huge difference in the over-all visual effects desired in a natural setting.

Color

Color at times can be a little tricky, but basically the colors of your materials need to be somewhat consistent with one another. At first appearance, a rock or boulder may look as if it is basically one color but upon careful examination you will find that there are literally dozens of shades and speckles and spots that make up the surface of most rocks. For this reason, the rock material you choose can vary to some extent but needs to be within the same range of colors. The fastest way for an out-of-place rock to stick out and be unnecessarily noticed is to change its color. If all of the rocks in your water feature have a reddish hue, you do not want a big white rock stuck in the middle and expect it to look like it belongs there. Remember that the rocks are typically structural or accent elements and not normally intended to be the focal point of your feature.

The same is true when you select any small stones, gravel or sand for your feature; they too need to be within the same range of colors. In nature, smaller rocks and gravel are just pieces that have been broken off of the larger surrounding boulders. There may be some slight variations because the gravel may be smooth and somewhat polished from tumbling action in the water but they are still smaller pieces of those same bigger rocks and should carry similar color combinations.

Character-lines

Character-lines are another aspect that can accent the phenomenal appearances in your naturalistic water features, adding tremendous interest and dimension. These character-lines are the small ridges, crevasses, folds and grooves you will find formed on the natural surface of many mountain stone varieties of rocks and boulders. Character-lines can enhance the significant overall appearance of the materials by introducing light and shadow to an otherwise smooth surface.

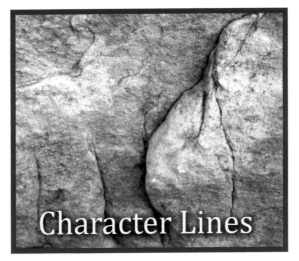

In other words, a rock with surface character will look much more interesting than a plain smooth rock. When used in conjunction with the movement of water in streambed and waterfall applications, these ridges and grooves can provide additional turbulence thereby enhancing the water hydraulics in your design, which directly affect the sights and sounds of the moving water.

The single most sought after quality in any water feature design is the resulting effect of its sights and sounds. Without the audible and visual effects, a water feature is no longer of interest.

Mosses

Lichens

Combined

Moss and Lichens

Moss and Lichens pre-existing on your rocks and boulders can add a dimension to your features that is not impossible but difficult to obtain on your own. It can take years to cultivate wild mosses and lichens on the surfaces of some rocks and boulders, depending on their composition and density. There are methods and techniques available that can be used to introduce these simplistic plant varieties to your rocks and boulders. Yogurt and buttermilk cultures work very well when mixed with moss varieties and then distributed on the surfaces of the rocks. This, of course, will get the mosses started but in no way guarantees the long-term existence of these plants.

If you can find and purchase your rock materials with these plants already growing on the surface, you have made a huge step forward in the achievement of natural results. The existence of mosses and lichens seems to give the boulders the appearance that they have been there since the beginning of time rather than having a sterile, washed out look from sitting in a landscape supply yard, baking in the sun. Sterile, lifeless rocks can distract from the overall appearance you desire.

The surface characteristics of the rocks and boulders used in any water feature will certainly play a large part in the over-all completed appearance of your projects. Texture, color and other surface anomalies can make a water feature appear to have been around for years rather than just having been recently installed.

Material Quantities

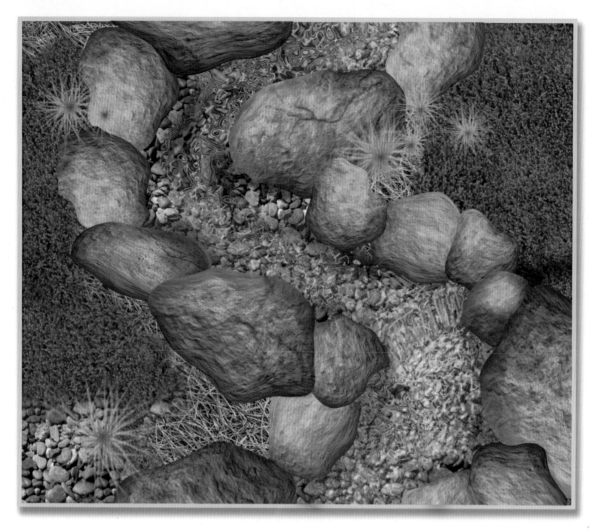

100% Rock

Using 100 percent rock edging has been a very prominent element in water features for many years. It was considered a very easy and inexpensive way to hide the liner. However, this is not the correct way to edge a water feature if you intend on achieving naturalistic results. Less than 40% of shorelines and stream banks found under natural conditions actually consist of large rock material.

Material Quantities

In nature, slightly more than one third of all pond shorelines and stream banks are made up of large rock material. Yet the vast majority of installed water features consist of 100% rock edging. If the rock material is all consistently the same small size, it will really take away from the natural appearance you are after. It can look somewhat better if the shorelines and stream banks have been constructed using large rocks and boulders of various sizes but 100% rock shorelines are still

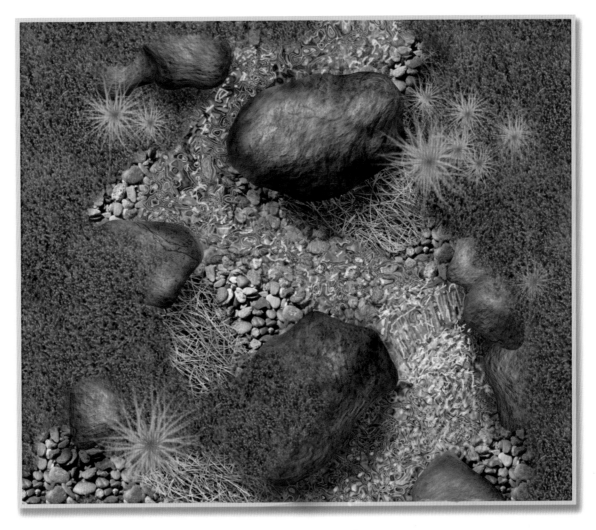

50% Rock

excessive and unnatural, regardless of the material size used. This method has no place in today's naturalistic water feature creations.

A very important part of making any water feature appear natural is to NOT allow the shoreline to contain more than 40% or 50% rock or boulder material. Huge moss-covered logs, driftwood, sandy beaches, gravel bars, planting beds, bog areas or even grass growing right to the water's edge are just a few of the other methods of edging a water feature, providing a more diverse and natural appearance to your projects.

The days of lining a water feature with an endless and monotonous row of rock material are over. It is time that more natural and visually appealing edging techniques are utilized in today's' water feature installations. No more than 50 percent of any shoreline should consist of rock edging if natural appearances are desired.

Approximately one third of naturally existing pond shorelines and stream banks are made up of large rock material, yet the vast majority of constructed water features consist of 100% rock edging.

CHAPTER

20

Man-Made Retaining Wall

Using stacks and stacks of small rocks piled meticulously on top of one another for the sake of concealing a steep slope at the edge of a water feature will not give you a nice natural appeal. These man-made retaining walls not only appear unnatural, they are not very stable or safe, and will use far more rock material and labor than is necessary.

Material Sizes

When rocks or boulders are being used in water feature applications, size really does matter and bigger is better. It is not difficult to learn proper techniques and procedures that will allow you to easily and safely place large rocks and boulders in your designed projects.

For some reason though, the decision to place hundreds or even thousands of smaller rocks stacked meticulously and

Single Boulder Outcrop

methodically around the waters edge is the preferable, yet unacceptable and totally unnatural choice of many who undertake a water feature project. This is one of the most noticeable mistakes and dramatic errors utilized in today's water feature installations. Not only is this an unsightly alternative, but it is also one of the most unstable and unsafe techniques used. This technique alone can completely destroy the appearance of an otherwise well-designed project.

A single boulder strategically placed at the edge of a pond or stream can provide stability and naturalistic appearances when trying to camouflage liner material on a steep slope. Not only will this provide the preferred natural result, it is also extremely easy to accomplish and very safe after installation is completed.

In addition, to being very unnatural and unsightly, it is usually not very cost effective. Not only will you purchase and use two to three times more rock than necessary, but you will also spend additional labor time placing all of these wasted materials. One single large boulder, or perhaps an artistic arrangement of two or three large rocks forming a nice rocky outcrop, simply looks more appealing and natural.

The R.I.S.E. Method can have so many profound and positive affects on your water feature projects. You will have fewer materials to purchase for your projects along with a substantial reduction in over-all costs for those materials. Because you have fewer materials, you will use less time placing those materials and end up with a safer, more user friendly water feature. You will also achieve a greater natural appearance in the resulting project.

Multi-Boulder Outcrop

An acceptable alternative to the single boulder outcrop is to use two or three large sized rocks or boulders and construct an attractive multi-rock structure that provides both naturalistic appearances and stability on the slope. These multi-rock outcrops can be staggered and terraced for visual appeal while still achieving all of the projects intended goals.

These numerous facts seem to be overwhelming odds in favor of a more productive installation method, yet the majority of water features installed completely ignore these facts.

Material Types

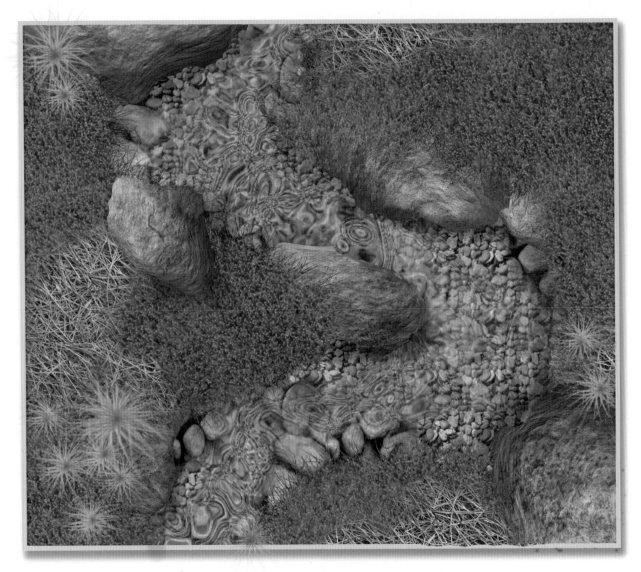

River Rock Streambed

It is important to understand what types of rocks to use in water feature
applications and where to place those particular varieties of rock. River
rock is created from surface friction and abrasive actions in the river
bottoms and has no place outside of streambeds. It is not found
naturally outside of this environment and should not be used
in these instances if natural results are desired.

Material Types

Using the correct types of materials in the appropriate applications is as different as night and day. It is not an issue of just selecting the correct sizes of materials used and placing them in the proper position for each application; it is also selecting the proper types of materials altogether.

A critical error found in some water feature installations is the use, or misuse, of the incorrect types of natural rock material. Having some knowledge about the geological formation of some of the different types of rocks available will be beneficial in selecting the correct choices for your water feature projects. A perfect example of this is the fact that rounded river rock is readily available most everywhere at a somewhat reasonable cost. Using this type of rock outside its natural environment can reduce the appeal of a natural appearance.

River rock is called by this name because it is found in the river bottoms and is round and smooth because it is constantly bombarded by sand and silt as it tumbles down the rivers and streams during peak water runoff periods. The moment it is removed from its natural surroundings and placed in a different environment, it immediately loses its natural characteristics and appeal. Rounded river rock should not be used as an edging material outside of the confines of water. It is not found naturally under these circumstances and it will not look like it belongs in these situations or applications, so simply don't use it if in fact you want to achieve natural results.

Another critical error made during installation involving the incorrect use of rock material in the wrong application would be the use of flat flagstone for waterfall construction. Flagstone is a sedimentary rock formation created in calm waters whereby suspended "sediment" in the water is allowed to settle to the bottom. Over a prolonged period of time, these deposits are compressed into rock by heat and pressure. Nowhere on this planet will you find flat (sedimentary) flagstone in the middle of a wild raging waterfall because it would simply dissolve and wear away over a relatively short period of time under such circumstances.

Flagstone Waterfall

Understanding a little about the various types of rock and how these rocks
are formed, will assist in the naturalistic creation of water features.
Sedimentary rocks such as flagstone are used many times for their ease of
distributing water across the weir of a constructed waterfall yet these
structures do not exist in the natural world because this sedimentary
substance would simply dissolve under the force of the flowing water.

Nor will you be able to find a combination of river rock edging along a stream bank topped by a flat flagstone waterfall, yet this is the method of construction utilized by those who did not bother to consult nature before they selected the materials for their project. Geologically you will not find these two rock formations in close proximity to one another under natural conditions. So once again the question is raised as to why we are installing our water features with these unnatural combinations while expecting to achieve natural results?

An additional reason in which installers are misusing flagstone for waterfall applications is the fact that it is flat; this feature makes it extremely easy to distribute the water evenly over the entire surface of the waterfall. The problem with this choice is that every waterfall begins to look like the last one. Spreading water evenly over a perfectly flat rock that has been perfectly leveled so that a perfect curtain of water is displayed perfectly over its entire surface just does not have a natural appearance. Everything is too clean and even and smooth and...*perfect!*

Another downside to this method is that a perfect curtain of water does not produce much sound, and that is one of the most sought-after reasons for water feature popularity. People love the sights and sounds of moving water. These wide, flat, flagstone waterfall weirs also take substantially more water to fill. This will usually require a larger pump, plumbing and additional electrical consumption to operate. Natural waterfall construction using the correct types of materials will use less water and yield better hydraulics thereby producing greater visual and audible effects.

A significant additional attribute to these efficient waterfalls is a lesser use of energy, making the entire system more "green" effective.

A critical error found in many water feature installations is the use, or misuse, of the incorrect types of natural rock material.

Material Shapes

Avoid Geometric Shapes

Removing all signs of human influences can be tedious, detail oriented work. This attention to detail must be attained at all levels of the project in order to reach full sensory satisfaction in naturalistic results. Selecting the correct materials and their shapes are no exception. Always avoid shapes that may contribute to human influenced results.

Material Shapes

Rocks and boulders make up a large part of most of today's water feature projects. Because of this, these rocks and boulders are usually quite visible. For this reason alone, you should try to make them blend in even more than normal so that they do not stick out quite so obviously. Your rocks and boulders should be structural elements and accents and typically not the center of attention. Remember, the entire focus is supposed to be the sights and sounds of the moving water; everything else should play a supporting role in achieving this goal. Always try to avoid neat, clean geometric shapes in your choices of rock material. If your rocks and boulders are perfectly round or too square or triangular in shape, they will give a very distinct connection to man-made qualities or attributes.

Always try to use rocks and boulders void of any visual reference to anything man-made. I have seen many constructed water features that look so unnatural and out of place because all of the rocks were consistently the same size and shape, leaving the appearance of a large, man-made retaining wall with an inefficient trickle of water running over its surface.

Try to have a wide assortment of shapes from flat or thin rocks to thick and chunky. Using materials with completely irregular shaping can assist you in achieving these results. These irregular shapes will greatly assist you in following the R.I.S.E. Method by allowing some of these materials to actually suggest where and how they need to be placed. No, these rocks and boulders do not actually talk to you, but they will let you know where and how they need to be placed if you will pay attention and keep an open mind.

Use Natural Shapes

The shape or configuration of these rocks will also suggest to you how they were found in nature. Try to continue this previous placement in your water features. Nothing will look more out of place than a rock that looks like it needs to go one particular way and it has been placed in a totally unnatural position.

The use of irregularly shaped materials will greatly assist in the over-all appearance of your completed project. This will help in the removal of straight, level, square and plumb attributes that will have less than satisfactory results in your finished projects. Irregularity will always give a more naturalistic appeal to any designed element.

Your rocks and boulders
should be structural
elements and accents
and typically not
the center of attention.

Edging Details

Edging Details

Edge dressing or otherwise cleaning-up and detailing the perimeter of your water feature projects can be critical to the over-all appearance of the end results. If you are not supposed to line the entire edge of your water features with rock material, what can you do to camouflage and sufficiently blend these areas? Concealing the liner can be very challenging without making it look like an obvious end to a structural component. The answer is to actually do anything you want to do; the sky is the limit and you can use your imagination to disguise these difficult areas. Some of the available options can be quite simple while others may be slightly more difficult to accomplish.

The point is, if it will provide a natural appearing end result, then try it. It should never be a question of "can I do this?" or "can I do that?" but rather "how" can I do it and be successful with the concept or idea. The following techniques are just a few of the possibilities that can be used in edging the perimeter of most any water feature.

Coping Shelves

Coping shelves, one of the more frequently used options in pond applications, involve placing a shelf slightly below the planned operational water level where various sized edging rocks or boulders can be placed in an effort to hide or camouflage the edge of the waterproof lining. This technique allows you to bring the water level up onto the rocks for a more natural appearing shoreline that is safely located within the confines of the liner. Soil is then back-filled behind these rocks to complete the process. It is important to know ahead of time which sizes of rock you intend on using so that the coping shelf can be excavated to the proper dimensions. These shelves must be compacted solid enough to support the weight of the rock material as well as having the width to accommodate the actual size of the rocks themselves. It is quite satisfactory to have some of the rocks extend partially over the edge of the shelf, providing ledges and overhangs to

the depths below. There should not be any issues with stability as long as you keep approximately two-thirds of the rock firmly supported on the coping shelf. These overhangs provide safe havens from potential predators for your aquatic inhabitants and add a dimensional level that is sure to increase the natural appeal of your projects.

Mossy Logs and Driftwood

Mossy logs and driftwood are great sources of natural materials that can be utilized in the edge dressing process providing a much needed break in the unnecessary repetitious use of rock material. Many times these logs or branches can be procured very easily and inexpensively or even free of charge if you have an area where you can go and safely gather these materials yourself. The use of mossy logs and branches or the use of driftwood will depend upon your specific design, the look you want to create and the environmental conditions that exist around your specific project area. Moss covered logs prefer cool shady areas that are rich in moisture whereas a piece of driftwood could handle most any climatic or environmental condition, including bright, harsh sunlight. Mossy logs tend to be very dense and heavy because of their moisture content from prolonged contact with the ground as opposed to driftwood that is generally lighter in weight and bleached out from prolonged exposure to the sun. You must remember that wood can float, so you need to be sure that you properly anchor these items in place when used in conjunction with any water feature project.

Planting Beds or Pockets

Planting beds or pockets can provide wonderful opportunities for displaying a variety of both aquatic and terrestrial plants. Because these planting beds are located within the confines of the liner, they will retain moisture very well. Raising or lowering the level of the soil or planting media within the planting bed can easily control the actual saturation level. A lower elevation will place the roots of the plants below the water level in the soil and a higher elevation will raise the plants up into a dryer environment. This will allow you to use a variety of plant combinations from fully aquatic specimens to some

terrestrial types that prefer moist conditions. This technique can provide some phenomenal combinations of plants that normally would be difficult to display together within the same area. These planting beds and pockets are a very unique way to disguise both the edges of your water feature as well as provide great focal points with your planting selections.

Bog Areas

Bog areas are technically classified as "contained mud holes." They are that point of existence hovering somewhere between dry land and open water and can be absolutely awesome focal points and a wonderful way to dress areas of edging that may otherwise be difficult to hide. Bog areas are noted for being able to house and sustain some very exotic varieties of plants. Of particular popularity are some of the carnivorous varieties, such as Pitcher Plants and Venus Flytraps. It is important to note here that a bog area needs to allow water to seep into and out of its containment. This is necessary to facilitate the existence of the "mud," but be sure that you do not allow the creation of any significant current that will stir the mud and cloud the water quality in your project.

Grassy Slopes

Grassy slopes can add a very nice change of pace to the edge of any water feature, particularly a pond. To have a nice, thick, lush section of grass growing right down to the waters edge just has an appeal to many people. Caution must be taken towards the actual variety of grass placed in this type of installation. Select a variety that will withstand a certain amount of excess moisture because water can wick up the face of the liner that partially extends under the grass. The distance the liner extends under the sod will be dependent upon the actual grade of the slope. The flatter the rise, the longer the liner should run. A good calculation to follow is to allow the liner to extend approximately four full inches above the operational level of the water. Notice that this method does not take into consideration how far the liner runs as long as it ends up at four inches above water level. Grassy slopes are always great focal points and the destination of choice for someone lying on the grass on a warm summer day.

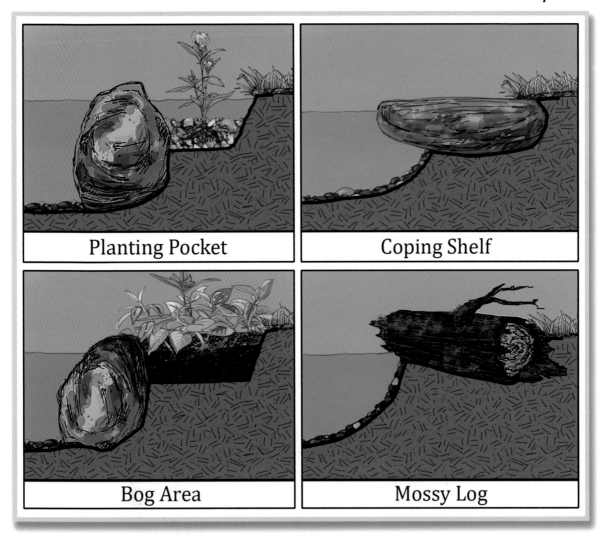

Planting Pocket

Coping Shelf

Bog Area

Mossy Log

Edging Details

Planted Beaches

Planted beaches can be very similar in structure to the grassy slope with the only difference being a selection of one particular type of plant or variety of plant species taking the place of the grass itself. The design and installation processes of these two methods are otherwise the same. Many plant roots do not "weave" themselves together into a tight mat, so caution must be taken that the slope of the beach area is not too steep causing the plants to become unstable and "slide"

The use of shelves and containment techniques will allow the installer a wide variety of options in providing adequate methods for hiding rubber liners and other types of water-proof membranes. Coping shelves for rock and boulder placement or large mossy logs and planting pockets can be quite successful ways to give a completely natural appeal to any water feature edge.

downhill on the liner base and into the water. This situation can be avoided if you allow a significant base for the plants to attach themselves to. A consideration here is to select a variety of plants that can handle both wet and dry root conditions since the liner base will slightly alter the moisture content from one section to another. Where the liner exists will obviously be moist and where the liner ends this moisture will be allowed to seep away, creating a dryer environment. There are many available plants that will handle these varied conditions quite well, allowing you to create some very interesting areas along the perimeter of your water features using this simple technique.

Gravel Bars

Gravel bars can make significant changes in appearance from landscaped areas and add a dimension to your features that truly shows nature's diversity. Keep in mind that most times when you see gravel bars in natural situations, they are typically located along streams where, during peak water run-off periods, fast-moving turbulent water has "pushed" the gravel up onto low lying areas in the surrounding landmass. Then, after this high water subsides, the gravel bars are left exposed on the stream banks. These gravel bars are very easy to install and maintain as well as being very useful as a camouflage technique for hiding those difficult liner edges. Remember to consider the conditions that would cause a gravel bar to exist naturally. In most cases they would be located on the outside edges of a significant turn in a stream or creek. A gravel bar located on the inside of a turn would not provide the necessary existence as a credible element.

Sandy Beaches

Sandy beaches can make some installers very nervous because they fear that the sand might move about and shift too freely, possibly causing damage to components like pumps and filters. This could not be further from the truth. A properly installed sandy beach rarely has any shifting issues of any kind and most good quality pumps on the market today have solids handling capabilities that would more than adequately handle an occasional free floating sand particle. The advantages of installing a nice stretch of sandy beach far outweigh any possible or potential threats to any components. Sand is available in a variety of types and sizes and a good,

Grassy Slope

Planted Beach

Sandy Beach

Gravel Bar

Edging Details

The use of gentle slopes and beach areas are another great way to successfully camouflage the edges of a water feature. Sand and gravel or grass and other plant material can adequately hide the outside perimeter of your constructed features while providing very natural appearances for viewers to enjoy.

heavy sand will simply stay put where you want it to be, provided you do not have a raging current ripping through the beach. The sanded areas all handle mild currents and wave action quite well.

The use of gentle slopes
and beach areas are
another great way to
successfully camouflage
the edges of a water feature.

Final Thoughts

CHAPTER

24

Final Thoughts

Remember, we as humans are blessed with an advanced level of intelligence, capable of deciphering anything. With this knowledge, we have the ability to accomplish or recreate nearly anything imaginable or unimaginable for that matter.

If you see a truly natural awe-inspiring water feature, you have the ability to completely replicate that scene. All you need are the correct tools, the right components, the properly selected materials and the desire to apply yourself while utilizing the necessary techniques that will culminate in the desired result. You should never say, "I can't do that!" but rather say, "How can I accomplish this?"

If you are serious in pursuing a career in the water feature industry, and specifically in quality water feature design and installation, do not ever think you have learned it all. Never stop attending training seminars or workshops and always keep an open mind. There is always new and innovative information that comes along in the form of publications, such as this one, or educational programs offered by industry leading manufacturers, or organizations. Take a responsible stand in supporting the industry that supports your efforts and career choice by joining a non-profit organization like the National Association of Pond Professionals.

This book has given you the techniques and methods necessary for accomplishing the task of recreating precisely naturalistic water features. The reasons why nature looks so natural, proper application of these detailed elements, and the reasons they work, have all been laid out for your use. Your success in quality naturalistic water feature installation rests firmly in your own hands.

You can advance as far as you want to in creating absolutely awesome landscape and architectural aquatic features. Pay attention to the details, use the best components and materials you can find, and above all do your very best and you can succeed!

Remember always; if you see it in nature, try it in your water features!

With Sincere Wishes for a Prosperous Future,

Index

Accepted Design Concepts 20

Algae Control 54

Algae Production...57

Angle of Descent 54

Aquatic Plants..................54, 60, 73, 78, 113

Audible Dimension........................72, 73 ,78

Bogs...95, 114

Borders 40, 41

Boulder Diversion 80

Boundaries....................................40, 41, 70

Centered 29

Character Lines 88, 91

Colors 20, 22, 88, 90–92

Confined Material Placements.....................40

Complex Island Structure............................65

Confined Material Placement 40

Contractor Surveys 26

Controlling Sound Direction........................77

Controlling Sound Volume 76

Coping Shelf.............................112, 113, 115

Critical Errors 103, 106

Deep Pool 54, 75, 76

Deep Water Canyon 52

Depth 51, 52, 54, 57, 70,
72-78, 80, 84, 86, 113

Design Concepts 20

(Design) Credibility 49, 83

Detailing 112

Dimensional Configuration.......................54

Directional Descent....................................82

Directional Flow 83

Driftwood 64, 65, 95, 113

Dissolved Oxygen......................................60

Diversions 64

Drops 49, 54, 64, 73, 74, 75

Echo Chambers 76, 77

Edge Dressing 112, 113

Edging Details.........................112, 115, 117

Educational Institution 8, 11

Effective Elevational Change 48

Elevational Contouring........................82, 83

Elevational Drop......................54, 73, 74, 75

Erratic 10, 44, 45, 88

Erratic Watercourse 46

Even Occurrences 36

Evenly Spaced Materials......................29, 37

Exaggerated Turns 60, 61

External Confinement...........................40

Fixed Course 44

Flagstone.................................103–105

Formation of Ice 54

Friction...........................53, 54, 69, 70, 102

Functional Surface.........................90–92

Fundamental Concepts 13

Geometric Shapes 108, 109

Grade Level 82

Grassy Slopes..................41, 114, 115, 117

Gravel Bars 95, 116, 117

Height 49, 86

High-Range Tones............................72, 74

High Ratio Movement 48, 69

Hydraulics.........................48, 60, 91, 105

Inferior Design 40

Inferior Installation Practices.....................13

Irregular 10, 36

Irregular Shapes 109

Irregularly Spaced Materials 37

Islands 64, 65

Low-Range Tones................................75, 76

Low Ratio Movement 68

Man-Made Influences................................29

Man-Made Retaining Wall..................98, 109

Material Placement....................33, 34, 40, 86

Material Quantities.................................94

Material Selection.........................18, 38, 90

Material Shapes.....................................108

Material Sizes.................................95, 98

Material Types............................ 40, 41, 103

Mid-Range Tones 74, 75

Moss and Lichens 92

Moss Covered Logs..............................113

Multi-Boulder Outcrop............................100

Index

Narrow Canyons 56

National Association of
    Pond Professionals...............8, 11, 121

Natural Appearances 18, 21, 24, 28, 33,
    40, 41, 49, 81, 83, 86, 94,
    95, 100, 103, 105, 112, 117

Natural Balance...20

Natural Designs...17

Natural (Naturalistic) Results...13, 17, 26, 29,
    56, 92, 94, 102, 103, 105, 108

Obstacles.......................44, 46, 64, 68, 82, 83

Outdated Installation Techniques...21, 22, 105

Patterned Material Placement 33

Pearl Necklace Effect 21, 32, 33

Planted Beach 115, 117

Planting Beds 65, 95, 113, 114

Planting Pockets.................................64, 115

Pools 52, 54, 72–76, 78

Proportionally Balanced 22

Random 10, 32, 83

Random Material Placement 34

Reasons for Change....................................80

Reconfigured Volume 53

River Rock 102, 103, 105

Rock Amounts 94, 95

Rock Diversions 64

Sandy Beach 95, 116, 117

Savio Water Feature Institute 8, 9, 11

Sedimentary Rock 103, 104

Shallow Areas 57

Shallow Pools 74, 75

Single Boulder Outcrop 99, 100

Slope Conditions 70

Slow Moving 57

Solid Surfaces 72–75

Sound 28, 54, 56, 57, 60, 68, 69,
72–77, 86, 91, 105, 109

Spacing Materials 36, 86

Specific Pattern 32

Speed 46, 53, 54, 57, 64, 65,
68, 69, 73, 80, 86

Splash Control 73–75

Splits 29, 64, 65

Spontaneous 10, 40

Spontaneous Material Placement 41

Stagnant Water 60

Straight Fixed Watercourse 44

Sufficient Current 60

Surface Separation 64

Textures 20, 22, 88, 90, 92

The R.I.S.E. Method 10, 13, 16–18, 21, 25,
26, 28, 34, 100, 109

Topographical Diversion 81

Turbulence 56, 57, 60, 69, 86, 91

Turns 44, 45, 60–62

Unnatural (Design) Appearances ...22, 32, 34,
36, 94, 98–100, 105, 109

Visual Enhancements 54

Volcano Effect 49

Water Loss 70, 73

Water Movement 57, 68, 72, 73, 82

Water Temperature 54, 57

Water Quality 24, 60, 114

Water Velocity 68–70

Water Volume 52–54, 57, 68, 69, 76, 82

Wide Areas 57

Wide Shallows 57

Width 29, 46, 56, 57, 80, 84, 86, 112

Wildlife (Habitat) 53, 54, 65, 72, 78

Winding Fixed Watercourse 45

List of Illustrations & Photo Credits

Illustrations

100% Rock.................................94

50% Rock..................................95

Accepted Design Concepts 20

Advancing Our Industry............................8

Avoid Geometric Shapes...........................108

Boulder Diversion 80

Complex Island Structure 65

Confined Material Placement 40

Controlling Sound Direction.......................77

Controlling Sound Volume..........................76

Controlling Splash 73

Deep Water Canyon 52

Edging Details, Part 1................................115

Edging Details, Part 2................................117

Effective Elevational Change 48

Elevational Contouring...............................82

Elevational Influences on Velocity 70

Erratic Watercourse 46, 129

Evenly Spaced Materials............................37

Flagstone Waterfall 104

High Ratio Movement 69

Irregularly Spaced Materials 37

Low Ratio Movement 68

Man-Made Design Influences 29

Man-Made Retaining Wall.........................98

Multi-Boulder Outcrop.............................100

Narrow Canyons..56

Over-Exaggerate Turns...............................61

Patterned Material Placement 33

Pearl Necklace Effect 32

Random Material Placement.......................34

Reconfigured Volume 53

River Rock Streambed 7, 102

Single Boulder Outcrop..............................99

Single Rock Diversion 64

Spontaneous Material Placement............7, 41

Straight Fixed Watercourse 44

The R.I.S.E. Method 16

The "Volcano Effect" 49

Topographical Diversion 81

Use Natural Shapes 109

Water Cuts Corners.................................... 61

Water Falling Into A Deep Pool 75

Water Falling Into A Shallow Pool 74

Water Falling On A Solid Surface................. 72

Wide Shallows.. 57

Winding Fixed Watercourse........................ 45

(All graphic illustrations and design formats were created and compiled by Shawn Hiser.)

Photo Credits

Rick Bartel, Instructor and Author............... 11
(Photograph provided by SWFI)

Excellence Through Education 12
(Photograph provided by Rhonda King, King Fotography)

Final Thoughts... 87
(Photograph provided by Rhonda King, King Fotography)

Natural Resulting Designs 17
(Photograph provided by Autumn Mist Aquatics)

Outdated Installation Techniques.........21, 105
(Photograph provided by SWFI)

Over 80% Prefer Natural 25
(Photograph provided by Autumn Mist Aquatics)

Rock Placement..87
(Photograph provided by Rhonda King, King Fotography)

Surface Characteristics
(Photographs provided by SWFI)
    Character Lines................................... 91
    Combined 92
    Lichens.. 92
    Mosses 92

Unnatural Appearances 22
(Photograph provided by SWFI)

Cover and Miscellaneous ....14, 30, 50, 66, 120, 121, 126, and 130
(Photograph provided by Rhonda King, King Fotography)